Living the Call

Volume 2
Mel & Corliss Erickson

Written by Karen Koczwara

The statements in this book are substantially true; however, names and minor details may have been changed to protect people and situations from accusation or incrimination.

Front cover photos and art work depicted on the cover are the property of the Ericksons.

Published in Beaverton, Oregon, by Good Book Publishing.
www.goodbookpublishing.com
V1.1

Printed in the United States of America

Melton H Erickson
Milton H Erickson

Table of Contents

Dedication

We want to dedicate this book, Volume 2 of *Living the Call,* to our adult children, their spouses and children. We dedicate it to our many grandchildren whom we love so much. Thanks for bringing so much joy into our lives! We also want to dedicate it to our brothers and sisters and their families. Thanks for playing a big part in our lives!

To our many friends and supporters of our ministry throughout the years we say thank you and dedicate this book to you. Without your support and prayers there would be no story to write of living out God's call. Thank you!

There are some stories that need to be told because they are stories of God's intervention in the affairs of men. To this end we give God the glory and thanks for the life he has given us, because it's really not about us, it's about God. It's about his love, care, guidance, protection and miracles in our lives. So we dedicate this book to the glory of God!

Foreword

Have you ever had a divine appointment? Today, walking down the street in Mexico, we ran into a man we witnessed to years before. What were the chances that on the very week we were in this Mexican city we would cross paths with this man once again? As we talked with him about his progress toward the Lord, we knew this was a divine appointment.

Living the Call, Volume 2 is an undeniable account of a godly man and wife moving daily from one divine appointment to the next. I lost track of the number of souls mentioned in this book led to heaven because of a flat tire here, a willingness to help there and a willingness to follow God's daily instructions. I can tell you this — if you were to keep track, you would find thousands!

How do you measure a man or woman of God? Today we like to measure them by who has the biggest TV following or the largest congregation. However, I am convinced it won't be that way in heaven. It will be he who dug the deepest into the hard soil of the land where God has placed him. These two faithfully served where most would never have considered — in humble places, in humble circumstances, but with a daily dose of God's miraculous in their lives.

This book will leave you laughing one moment and in tears the next. It will bring you face to face with God as he confronts you with the question: Are you ready for divine appointments? Are you humble enough to do anything he asks of you? Are you willing to be prayed up and ready when that moment comes?

David Boyd
National BGMC Director
Assemblies of God

Acknowledgements

We would like to acknowledge some of the people who have been influential in the writing of this book. As missionaries, we receive support from the body of believers. We would like to thank each one who has given and prayed so that God's work can be accomplished.

MAPS teams and MAPS RVers have worked with us during construction projects. Without their help and that of the many volunteer teams who came, there would not be a story to tell about churches being built.

We gratefully acknowledge the people who worked with us on Conquest Outreaches. Their help was significant in the spreading of the gospel and the salvation of souls. Many received the call of God on their own lives through the impact of these outreaches.

We once again want to acknowledge our family and friends who will be a part of our lives forever. Our family is a special part of our lives. We have made many friends across the nation in many churches during itineration. We look forward to sharing this entire story with you through the printed page.

Thank you, Daren Lindley. Good Book Publishing Company has been excellent to work with. Peter Bell, our project manager: You get a big A+! You were so patient with us and always with a wonderful Christian attitude. How many e-mails did we send back and forth?! You encouraged and inspired us to keep on working and gave priority to excellence.

Karen Koczwara, you deserve our greatest thanks for all the phone calls and the writing of the original manuscript. Thanks for allowing us to tweak, change, add and subtract so that the story could be written with authenticity as it really happened.

Thanks to Nathan and Evan who worked on the pictures in the book and the cover that we chose. We would be amiss not to thank the guys at Computer Hobbies right here at home for easily arranging all our pictures together for the cover.

God is the author of life, and we humbly acknowledge his direction and guidance. His wisdom is the practical side of problem solving. With his help, all things can be accomplished.

Introduction

The story continues: It's about a farm boy from North Dakota and a gal from northern Minnesota who met at North Central Bible College in Minneapolis with a call of God present on their lives. The following two decades of our lives have been as interesting as the decades of our lives in Volume 1. But it's really not about us — it's about God!

We hope you have read Volume 1 as well. Here's what readers are saying:

"It is quite a book ... very inspirational!" – *Orville*

"I sat up 'til 2 in the morning reading it." – *Rhonda*

"It's an engaging, faith-inspiring story." – *Darrin*

"It's precious, awesome!" – *Dan M.*

"It's cool!" – *Lori*

"Your story blessed my heart. Thanks for writing it!"
– *Kenneth W.*

"I love it!" – *Sharon*

Living the Call

"What an inspiring, God-honoring book, not to mention the fact that it was carefully written and professionally put together and published." – *Dan J.*

About Volume 2, a reader has said, "Fantastic book! I'm halfway through … I'm waiting to see if you come out of your coma!" – *David B.*

God is faithful. We want to give him the glory for everything he has done in and through our lives as related in the story of this book. Our children have grown up and given us grandchildren. Many people have met Christ through our Conquest Outreaches and ministry on Indian reservations throughout the United States. Many have gone on to win others to the Lord and find their own ministries. Church construction building projects have become vehicles for the gospel to be spread. This is a book of documentation of miraculous healings, miracles and ministry, in season and out of season!

The writing of this book is like a mandate to us from God. There are stories of angelic visitations in time of need that have not been told before. We hope you will be inspired to believe that God is real and watching over you all the time, caring about every detail of your life. Be inspired to know that, whatever God has for you to do, he will be with you, giving you the strength and opportunities to accomplish it.

Chapter One
Thanks, I Needed That

"I need to speak with you for a moment." The doctor looked grave as he moved into a separate room with my wife, Corliss.

"Yes?" Corliss looked into his eyes anxiously, bracing herself for bad news.

"Your husband's condition is serious. In all honesty, there is only a 10 percent chance he is going to live. If he does survive, he will be a vegetable for the rest of his life with only a 10 percent chance of complete recovery." He cleared his throat. "I'm sorry. If I were you, I would go home and start making preparations."

Preparations. Corliss lowered her eyes to the floor, unable to believe the doctor's words. This wasn't the first time she'd been told her husband might not live. But this was a dire situation. Viral encephalitis, the doctor had said: a rare but life-threatening infection causing inflammation of the brain. Most victims didn't survive. Corliss' heart beat quickly as she processed the terrible news.

"Again, I'm sorry," the doctor repeated, sighing sadly. "There's not much more we can do."

With a newfound determination, Corliss shook her head fiercely. "Doctor, I have six teenagers at home. I cannot raise them without my husband. I cannot lose him. I am going to pray and ask God for that slim chance of a complete recovery. I will call and ask people to pray."

The doctor frowned slightly. "Okay," he replied slowly.

"I will pray that God will heal my husband." In the quiet of that room, as down the hall machines beeped, doctors barked out orders and nurses called for assistance, Corliss began to pray. There was only one thing on her mind. She was desperate and determined that God would heal her husband, that she would not be a single mother left to raise six children alone.

"God, I've nearly lost Mel before, and you've spared his life. Would you please work a miracle again today? We need a miracle, God. Please heal my husband. Please, Lord."

કે કે કે

The beginning of the 1980s marked many interesting cultural changes. Pop music replaced rock and roll, fashion took on a bright, funky look and the microwave came into our kitchens. But on the little reservation in Tokio, North Dakota, many more exciting things were taking place. God was working in remarkable ways, people were coming to Christ every week and lives were being changed dramatically. Though Corliss and I had faced many challenges physically, spiritually and financially over the past decade, we were looking forward to embracing the future. Life, it seemed, was good.

Thanks, I Needed That

We were a family of eight. Corliss and I now had six children: three biological daughters, Shawna, Rhonda and Lynelle, and three adopted children, Michael, Ted and Brenda. They were all within a seven-year span of each other. God had provided us with a wonderful new home on the reservation, and our rapidly-growing children filled that home with life and laughter, teasing and activity. While Shawna, the oldest, remained the peacemaker, Rhonda and Michael had to be separated at the supper table to keep them out of mischief! As Lynelle, our youngest, started school in Warwick, Shawna made sure she got to her classroom, and the older kids looked out for her on the bus. The kids became active in sports, joining basketball and baseball teams at school. Their games took up a great deal of our time, and we loved every minute of it. An avid sports fan and player myself, I was glad to see our children excelling in and enjoying sports, to say nothing about the swimming lessons Corliss brought them to, band in school, play practice, summers at camp working in the cafeteria or attending as campers. The older kids watched over the younger ones.

Outside our home, things were moving forward as well. Our little church, which had once had an attendance of just a couple dozen people, had now grown to new numbers. Each week, new families came to church, and many of them gave their hearts and lives to Jesus Christ. As exciting as it was to see our kids excel at basketball, it was even more thrilling to watch a life transformed by the power of the Lord. Many of the Indians had been involved in promiscuous, drunken lifestyles when we arrived at the reservation in 1967. Few of them had held jobs, and even fewer owned homes. Due to the amazing work of God, we had seen hundreds of lives changed during our ministry thus far. Never in my life could I have imagined what God had in mind when he called me to the Indians as a young man.

In the spring of 1983, the Lowell Lundstrom Crusades came to Devil's Lake. These crusades were perhaps one of the most exciting events that took place near the reservation in all our years of ministry. Lowell and Connie Lundstrom had been country music singers before they committed their lives to Christ. After getting saved, they began traveling around the country in various forms of transportation but ended up traveling in buses converted into motor homes, conducting crusades, rallies and seminars. Lowell served as president of Trinity Bible College in North Dakota for a time and had a popular radio broadcast as well. When we learned his crusades were coming our way, we could hardly wait to invite the Indian people to attend. Many people had made decisions for Christ at the Lowell Lundstrom Crusades, and we prayed as a result there would be a revival on the reservation as well.

Every night we drove a busload of Indian people to the crusades where Lowell and his wife and team presented the message of salvation with anointed lively music and a powerful gospel message. His humor, stories and passion for the Lord touched many people. At the end of the crusade, 137 people from the reservation had come forward to accept Christ! Many I recognized as Indians who had once hardened their heart to any idea of religion or church. I had the privilege of leading the follow-up Bible studies and charismatic prayer services on Friday nights. Later, we followed up with each person, visiting them in their homes and asking if they had any questions about the Christian faith. It was a wonderfully exciting time.

We had been inviting people all over the reservation to the crusade. One Sunday evening we went to the service, hoping that one of the families we had invited would come. The dad in the family loved music but was not interested in coming to church. He had been baptized as a baby, and he said that was all he needed. That Sunday evening they showed up at the crusade, and when the crusade team gave the altar call, he and his family, holding hands, walked forward to the altar to accept Christ. A conversion of transformation took place, and the next Sunday they showed up in church. He read the Bible through in just a short time. They became an influential family working in the church as leaders, teachers and helpers in all areas. We appreciated them greatly.

As the church continued to grow, we invited special speakers to come and share with the congregation on the weekends. One of our speakers was Wes Bartell. He was at the house with us one evening when someone came with a young, pregnant Indian woman in the car who had swallowed a chicken bone, which was lodged in her windpipe. She was barely able to catch her breath.

"A chicken bone! I swallowed a chicken bone!" she said in a muffled, panicked voice.

Wes and Corliss rushed out to the car to the young woman's side. Wes was not only a wonderful man of God but a certified EMT as well. "We've got to dislodge that bone before she stops breathing!" he cried.

"Can we do the Heimlich maneuver on a pregnant woman?" Corliss asked with concern.

"We have to!" Wes replied. He and Corliss, also a licensed nurse, worked together to dislodge the chicken bone from the woman's throat. After a minute or two, the young woman let out a gasp of relief.

"I think we got it," Corliss said to the young woman after taking a deep breath. "You need to get to the hospital, though, to make sure you and the baby are okay."

Wes and I drove her to the hospital, and indeed the woman was okay. We praised God that he had brought together a nurse (my wife!) and a certified EMT at the very moment the woman needed help. It was always a pleasure to have guest speakers, but it was even more exciting when God used them in practical ways.

Another evening, a young Indian man from the church rushed to our house, a tiny baby in his arms. The baby was turning blue and in obvious distress. "Help me! Help my baby! He's not breathing right!" the man cried frantically.

Corliss dropped everything to assess the dire situation. "We have to do CPR right now," she told him, not stating the inevitable: ... *or he will die!* She showed the man how to do some delicate CPR on the baby on the front steps of our house until it began breathing and color returned. The baby lived and went on to be fine. Death was not uncommon on the reservation; fights, suicide and poor health due to drinking were among the common causes. But a newborn baby fighting for his life was a frightening sight. Thanks to Corliss' quick thinking and nursing skills and God's intervention, that baby lived. Little did she know that just a few years later another life-and-death situation would hit even closer to home.

One evening some of the neighbors down the street had gotten into it with each other, taking out revenge on one of the young teenagers by beating him up. His friend helped him come to our house for refuge, shots ringing out above their heads as they ran. He dragged Ricky into our garage and laid him down. Corliss checked his pulse to make sure he was still alive. Inside the house, shots pinged above us as they hit the roof. The kids ducked down below the living room windows as if they were in an action movie before some of them retreated to the basement for safety. Eventually the police arrived, drove into the swamp across the street from our house and got stuck trying to apprehend the offender. The ambulance came and took Ricky to the hospital. After it was all over, the neighbors gathered around in our front yard, breathing a collective sigh of relief. Later our good friend Gladie asked us laughingly, "So did you serve coffee and cookies then?" Such was life sometimes on the reservation!

Living the Call

One of the more exciting things during our ministry was giving young Bible school students a chance to speak at our church. An exceptional young man, Dobie Weasel, a Sioux Indian from Montana, was one of them. He attended Trinity Bible College in North Dakota and came to speak at our church many times in the 80s. We were impressed by his speaking ability and dynamic preaching. With his charismatic personality, he interacted well with the congregation. We were glad he could "cut his teeth," so to speak, with us at our church in Tokio as he moved on into his future preaching ministry. I hoped that many of the Indians who had made decisions to attend Bible college would one day stand in the pulpit as well.

Our friends Jon and ReNelle also came to visit. ReNelle attended North Central Bible College in Minneapolis the same time as Corliss and I did. Jon directed a 24-person singing group called the Celebrant Singers and hailed from California. After the group sang in Tokio and nearby Fort Totten and picnicked at Sully's Hill, we housed everyone overnight at our place. The girls all piled their sleeping bags in the basement of our house, and the boys hunkered down in the church. Once again, I was thankful for the extra space God had provided for us in the new house. We'd had the opportunity to take in foster children, guest speakers, singers and visiting friends alike. There was never a dull moment in the Erickson household.

I performed many funerals and wakes on the reservation. The circumstances surrounding these events were unfortunate, but they were a wonderful opportunity to share the gospel message with those who mourned their loved ones. I remember Harry's funeral — Harry, who had seemed so unlikely to become a Christian with his background of sin! He got saved and became one of the first advisory board members of our church. After a couple years, Harry was hospitalized with a heart attack. His family was at the hospital one evening when they called me to come. I spent time with them, and we prayed for Harry's recovery. The family left, but Harry asked me to stay longer. He wanted to talk to me. He told me that he had been shown he was going to die and would not leave the hospital.

I told him, "The Lord is going to heal you."

Harry replied, "No, that is not going to happen." He asked me to have his funeral and to tell his friends and family that he wanted them to accept Christ as their Savior just as he had. If he had wronged others, he wanted them to forgive him, and he had forgiven all for anything they had done to him.

The next morning at 4:30 the phone rang. It was the hospital asking me to get his wife and come to the hospital because he had had a massive stroke. Within a matter of hours he died and went to be with his Lord and Savior. In the days following, we found out that Harry had been married before and had seven other children besides the six he had with his present wife. The next Sunday six of the oldest children were in church, and at the close of the service they all came forward and accepted Christ! I went to Fargo to meet the oldest son coming home from the military for his dad's funeral. I told him that his brothers and sisters had accepted Christ that morning in church and explained the way of salvation to him. He said, "Will you please stop the car so I can accept Christ before I die?"

Over the next two days people came from all across North Dakota, South Dakota and Montana for the wake and the funeral to show their respect for Harry. As he had asked, I preached salvation messages at both the wake and the funeral. More than 300 people accepted Christ as Savior because of the testimony that Harry asked me to share with the people before he died!

In 1983, many of the men from our church attended a men's retreat in Red Willow for a weekend. It was a wonderful time of fellowship, teaching, praying and praise. Events like this were especially exciting because in the first years our church had been filled with only women and children. To see men, the leaders of the home, coming to church and giving their lives to Christ was an answer to our prayers. One by one, these men gave up their vices, from drinking to cigarettes to promiscuity. Only God could get the credit for such transformation.

Through our ministerial meetings on the reservation, Corliss and I developed a relationship with Sister Nancy, a nun from the local Catholic church at Fort Totten, and with two of the priests. They became good friends of ours, and we enjoyed visiting with them whenever we could.

One day the two priests came to me, excited to talk about the things God was doing in the lives of the people. I invited them into our home on Saturday nights, and we began to discuss the miracles and transformed lives we'd seen in the ministry. We began to pray together for our churches. The priests had been filled with the Holy Spirit at a charismatic conference. The drapes of our living room were wide open for all to see: a pastor, his wife, a nun and two priests all praying together. I imagine it must have been quite a sight for anyone who happened to walk or drive by! What a wonderful reminder that, despite our differences, we served and loved the same God and could pray to him in unity.

We learned about an interesting program taking place at the Fort Totten Community School. The Catholic church had been holding release-time programs for the children after school. Priests would come into the classrooms for an hour after school ended and share the things of God with the children. Eventually, all the churches of the reservation had the opportunity to do release-time classes. After a year or so, it was Corliss and I who continued to conduct them. What an exciting opportunity!

Every Thursday we held these classes in one of the classrooms of the public school. Corliss taught the younger children, while I worked with the older ones. Many children filled the seats, eager to listen to the Bible being taught and coming to an understanding of the nature of God. We talked about everything from creation to the return of the Lord. They viewed the visual aid with interest, asking to know more. When the hour ended, they moaned, disappointed that it had passed so quickly. These release-time classes became one of the highlights of our ministry, and we thanked God for allowing us to reach children in the public school who might not otherwise have heard the gospel. Many of the children went on to attend our church and even bring their parents.

The early 80s brought about many new opportunities in our youth programs as well. Royal Rangers and Missionettes remained two popular afterschool programs for the Indian children on the reservation, in addition to Sunday school with its visual aid Bible stories and Vacation Bible School. We organized outings for the youth: hayrides, skating parties, Bible quizzes or showing thought-provoking Christian films in the church. One of the most important film series we showed our youth was the *Thief in the Night* series, which portrayed what might happen after the rapture. The young people were intrigued by these films and wanted to make sure their lives were right before God so that they might not be left behind if Jesus returned.

Many of the kids attended summer Bible camps, where they gave their hearts to the Lord or strengthened their existing relationship with him. Youth conventions in Fargo were another exciting event. Many children came back visibly energized for the Lord, and some were even filled with the Holy Spirit at a very young age. Nothing was more thrilling than seeing the next generation invested in the things of the kingdom of God.

"I think we are going to need more workers in the

youth programs at our church," I told Corliss one evening. "I can't believe how much it has grown."

"I agree," Corliss said. "We should start praying God will raise up more teachers."

God was always so faithful to meet our needs. More people began helping in Sunday school and the youth programs, taking some of the load off Corliss and me. It was rewarding to see Indians who had not long ago given their lives to Christ stepping up to serve in our church.

With so many wonderful things happening on the reservation, it was sometimes easy to forget that the enemy was still always at work, plotting, scheming, trying to snuff out the good. Each life that was given to Christ was one less he could hold in the palm of his evil hands. And in the winter of 1985, Satan made another grand attempt to kill, steal and destroy.

It was a chilly February, and Corliss and I had made dental appointments for our entire family in the town of Bismarck on Monday, Presidents' Day. We drove out to Bismarck on Sunday evening and stayed at a local hotel. Because we had such a large family, it was easier to tackle all of our appointments at once rather than make separate trips. We started early and stayed long.

On Monday morning, I woke up with a terrible headache. I tried to brush it off and gathered all the kids for the dentist appointments. At approximately 2 p.m., we headed home. Michael, now a freshman in high school playing varsity basketball, had a game that evening, and we were all looking forward to watching. Going to the children's sporting events was always a highlight of our family life. We encouraged the siblings to support one another at their various games; sometimes they were the players, sometimes the spectators.

As I drove the van, the children all fell asleep one by one. Eventually, Corliss nodded off, too. My head continued to pound, but I tried to ignore it. We had had a busy day, and I didn't want to miss out on one of Michael's last games of the season.

We made it safely to the game, and I continued to massage my throbbing head. The bright lights, blaring music and scuffling tennis shoes on the court were nearly too much for me to bear. It felt like a large drum was pounding over and over in my head. Halfway through the game, I stumbled to the corner of the gym, where I sat down on one of the sports mats and bent over in agony. Normally, I enjoyed every minute of Michael's games; I was a tall Swede who couldn't jump very high, but Michael was 5 feet, 9 inches and could dunk it with both hands. So I could hardly wait to get to the gym and watch him play each time.

But tonight, after what felt like the longest basketball game in history, we returned home. Corliss had to go to work at the nursing home in Devil's Lake where she worked as a nurse three times a week. I went to bed and asked Corliss, "Please, honey, can you get me a couple Tylenol? I'll go to sleep and be okay by morning." I had had some headaches in my life, but this one trumped them all. I don't remember much after that moment.

Thanks, I Needed That

That night at work, Corliss had a foreboding experience as she walked into one of the empty rooms. She felt there was a man who was covered in a shroud of darkness. It was frightening, but she didn't know what it meant.

In the morning, Shawna and Rhonda came to my room and asked me a question, only to get an answer that didn't make sense. Corliss returned home, and I was talking out of my head. They weren't able to understand me. I was delirious. "Mel! Mel! Talk to me! What's wrong?" she said with apprehension. "Mel! Do you still have a headache?"

I mumbled an incoherent answer as I slipped into a semiconscious state. Corliss said to the girls, "We need to call the ambulance to get Dad to the hospital." I was rushed to Mercy Hospital in Devil's Lake.

Everything went into fast forward when we arrived at the hospital. I was still delirious, mumbling strange things and staring off into space. "We'll run some tests and see what's going on with your husband," the doctor told Corliss, wheeling me back past the emergency room.

Corliss stayed by my side as the doctors worked quickly to assess my situation. It was clear something was terribly wrong, and it seemed to be stemming from my brain. Nightfall came, and I was not getting better, but worse. I continued to remain delirious, drifting in and out of sleep. Corliss stayed in the room near me, trying to rest on a cot. But I looked at her as if I had never seen her before. In the morning, the doctors made a decision: I

Living the Call

needed to be taken to another hospital in Grand Forks.

"I need your help for a few days," Corliss said wearily to my parents after making a few phone calls. "Can you come stay with the kids? Mel is in the hospital, and it's very serious."

I was no stranger to hospitals. Starting with my life-threatening tractor accident at age 14, I'd been in and out of the emergency room for everything from a minor car accident to a major stroke. God had spared my life time and time again. Corliss had remained the ever-faithful, strong wife. This, however, was frightening on a new level. No one had been able to determine the cause of my symptoms, and I was only growing worse. Was it too late this time?

United Hospital was located in Grand Forks, 85 miles east of Devil's Lake. My parents arrived at home to take care of our children, allowing Corliss to stay with me for the next few days. I thrashed in my bed delirious while she waited and prayed by my side. Concerned doctors and nurses flitted in and out of the room to check on me, still baffled by my condition. They continued to run tests, trying to pinpoint the problem.

In the Intensive Care Unit, the doctors attempted to put a stomach tube down my throat. I was so delirious that I grew agitated and bit the top of the stomach tube right off, leaving the other half in the bewildered doctor's hands.

At last, that Friday, Corliss got an answer. I had been stricken with acute viral encephalitis, a very serious

Thanks, I Needed That

inflammation of the brain. The doctors told her I had a 10 percent chance of survival. In the past month, there had been half a dozen other cases of this virus reported in North Dakota, and only one of the victims had survived. Corliss winced at the news and then resolutely declared to the doctor that she would pray and call on everyone she knew to pray for God to heal me completely. She said, "I have six teenagers at home. I cannot raise them by myself!" The doctors shrugged; what could it hurt? At this point, I'd been all but declared dead.

Corliss called up the District of Assemblies of God, her family members and everyone she knew for prayer. I am certain that within minutes, prayers from people all over the country went straight up to heaven. As I continued to drift in and out of consciousness, a God who never sleeps leaned down from heaven and listened.

After spending an hour or so with God, giving her husband to the Lord but asking him to spare me, Corliss walked into the Intensive Care Unit at noon. I looked up at her and began talking normally! A miracle was taking place. I asked, "May I please have a glass of water?"

You have never seen anyone respond so quickly to a man simply asking for a drink of water! Within seconds, a team of astonished doctors rushed to my bedside, staring at me incredulously. "Someone get the man a glass of water!"

"Could I brush my teeth, too?" I asked. "And maybe have some toast and 7-Up? And I need to use the restroom." It was then that I looked down and saw the restraints on my hands and feet. What on earth had happened to me?

"Can someone get him some toast and 7-Up?" The doctors were still scratching their heads, unable to believe that a man who had spent the last week in a semiconscious or delirious state was now sitting up in bed, asking for a glass of water as though nothing had happened at all.

Over the course of the day, things became clearer to me. Though I was still groggy, I was able to think semi-coherently and process the events that had led me to this hospital bed. The last thing I'd remembered was asking for a couple of Tylenol; everything had gone black after that. Now here I was, coming back from the brink of death, as the doctors said. Nurses buzzed in and out of my room, checking my monitors, bringing me food and necessities, with doctors trying to figure out just how I had come out of this critical stage so quickly! More than one doctor had all but declared me dead. At best, they'd said I would be a vegetable. And now I was sitting up in bed conversing with them! It was truly a miracle of God.

"What are these chains doing on my hands and feet?" I asked the doctors.

"You were thrashing around so badly in your bed that we had to restrain you with those," the doctors explained. "At one time, we had five or six people trying to hold you down. You were very delirious."

Corliss and I praised God together. I had been stricken by acute viral encephalitis, and my condition had been quite grave. She said that the doctors had even encouraged

Thanks, I Needed That

her to go back and plan my funeral. But she'd said that she had six teenagers at home, and she couldn't raise them by herself. Once again, in what could only be described as a miracle, God had spared my life.

Seventy-two hours after I gained consciousness, the doctors agreed to send me home. They did a spinal tap on me before I left. I slept 21 to 23 hours a day for the first couple of weeks. My body was still extremely weak, and I had a long way to go in my recovery process. It would be months, the doctors said, before I would be back to my old self.

Two weeks after I was discharged, I returned to the clinic for an assessment. "I just still cannot for the life of me understand how you recovered so quickly," the doctor said, staring at me in amazement. "You had one of the more serious cases of viral encephalitis I've ever seen, and yet you're sitting here in front of me as though you'd never been on your deathbed. It amazes me."

I smiled, for I knew exactly how I had gotten well. God had granted me his healing power once again.

"We are going to give you an IQ test in a few weeks and run some other tests on you as well to see if your levels have returned to normal," the doctor continued.

I leaned forward, still smiling. "Doctor, promise me one thing. If all my tests come back normal, I want you to write in my chart: 'It was a miracle of God.' Can you do that?"

The doctor stared at me for a moment. "Okay," he shrugged.

Living the Call

As I headed home that day, I couldn't help but guess that the doctor was only humoring me. Would he really be bold enough to write that statement if all my tests returned as normal?

I went back home and continued to sleep for hours at a time. I was still very weak and had a bit of trouble with my memory, but overall, I was slowly returning to my old self and gaining back strength. Four weeks later, I returned to the clinic, where the doctors ran a variety of tests, including a spinal tap, blood work, a personality test, an IQ test and an electroencephalogram. They then wheeled me in a reclining wheelchair back to the office, where the doctors prepared to assess the tests.

"This is just amazing," the doctor said, shaking his head as he went over the results in his hands. "Everything has come back completely normal. This is unheard of. You went through quite an ordeal. Your initial spinal tap a few weeks ago was very cloudy, and this one came back totally normal. Unbelievable."

"You don't want to put your fingers next to that man's mouth," one doctor told another. "He bit off the top of the stomach tube when we tried to put it down his throat!"

I was not shocked. I had a personal relationship with a God who had parted the Red Sea, raised people from the dead and made wine from water. That same God was alive and present today and had healed me in a miraculous way.

"This is even more unbelievable to me," the doctor went on. "We have a copy of your IQ test here, and after comparing it to an IQ test you took some time ago, it looks like you have gone up seven points!"

I laughed. "Thanks! I needed that," I chuckled.

"You got well too quickly. You should have been in intensive care for three weeks, not just three days! I just don't know what to say." The doctor continued to stare at the papers as though he must have read something incorrectly.

"What is impossible with man only enters the realm of possibility with God," I replied boldly. "You promised that if my tests came back normal you would write on my chart 'It was a miracle of God.' Are you going to do that now?"

The doctor nodded, poised his pen and wrote the exact words on my chart. It was exciting to see a man who had spent 10 years in medical school acknowledge that only God could get the credit on this case.

I soon learned that the only other surviving case of viral encephalitis in the state was a girl who had had to undergo intensive speech therapy and physical therapy to walk again. The fact that I did not have any major long-term side effects of the illness other than some slight memory problems was a testimony to God's hand on my life and his attentive ear to the many who had prayed for me during my illness.

Two months after I came home, the people from church began asking if I would come to speak to them about what had happened. I was still very weak, and the day that I agreed to speak at the church, they carried me over to the building. I sat in a chair on the platform and shared my incredible story for 10 minutes. It was the most physical exertion I'd had since my ordeal, and when I got home that night, I slept for 26 hours straight!

Slowly, I returned to the pulpit and began speaking again. I was so thankful for the many people who had stepped in to help preach, lead and work in the Sunday school classrooms during my absence. It was a wonderful opportunity to praise God and give him all the glory for his healing work.

Life returned to normal, or as normal as it could possibly be for a preacher, his wife and six kids on an Indian reservation. Each day, I gained more and more of my strength back, and each day, I gave God all the glory. Satan had been so eager to snuff out my life and our ministry time and time again, but God had not allowed it. Though being in the ministry often presented challenges, I had to believe that God was at work every day, that we were exactly where he wanted us. And because he had spared my life again, I had to believe that he had a great work ahead for me, too.

Chapter Two
The Move

As the saying goes, "All good things must come to an end." In 1986, Corliss and I began praying about moving on from the reservation. We'd had little idea what to expect when we came to Tokio nearly 20 years before, but God had worked in ways we could not have imagined. We had come to love the Indian people as family, and the feeling seemed to be mutual. However, we both began feeling the tug on our hearts and believed that God might be closing this chapter in our lives.

Our children were now becoming teenagers; our oldest were approaching adulthood. Shawna would graduate high school the following summer and talked about attending Trinity Bible College. It was hard to believe that the little girl who had come into the world just weeks before we left for the reservation was now growing into a beautiful young woman almost ready to head off on her own.

The children's activities took up a great deal of our time on the reservation. Shawna, Rhonda, Michael and Lynelle all took piano lessons for a time; swimming, basketball, softball, school plays and band rounded out their busy schedules. Corliss and I enjoyed attending every possible game, giving them our loyal support. Though our ministry kept us busy, family always remained our first priority.

Over the years, snow skiing had become one of our favorite family activities. My sister Irene and her husband, Charlie, lived in Colorado Springs, Colorado. We enjoyed visiting them and learned to ski on the slopes of Breckenridge. My father grew up skiing in Sweden, and I was determined to follow in his footsteps. After an initial semiprivate lesson, Corliss and I became good skiers and tried to keep up with the older kids as they whizzed by us down the mountain in a blur of white powder. Grandma Erickson babysat Lynelle before she was old enough to learn to ski.

One particular winter, we went to Grand Rapids, Minnesota, to ski with my sister Maurine and her family. Aunt Maurine watched Lynelle as she hopped on her tiny skis and took off down the smaller hills in front of our condo, while the rest of us set out to enjoy the bigger hills. I considered myself a rather good skier by this point and was looking forward to a full day of flying down the slopes.

As I headed down the mountain with my brother-in-law, Tom, we got too close to each other, and our skis crossed. I fell backward, hitting my head, and everything went fuzzy. Not long after, I found myself in the hospital, unable to remember who I was or where I had been.

"So what happened? Was anyone hurt?" I asked, rubbing my eyes in confusion as I sat up in my hospital bed. "Do I live in Tokio? Do I have any kids?" My eyes focused on Corliss' face, and I frowned. "Are you my wife?"

"Yes, I am your wife, Corliss," she replied, looking concerned.

I continued to repeat these questions over and over throughout the day. I had suffered a concussion from my fall and could not remember a thing about my life. Our friends Bob and Judy, who pastored a church nearby in Grand Rapids, came to the hospital to be with us. They prayed over me, asking God to heal me and bring me out of the effects of this concussion. Maurine and Tom watched over the children while Corliss sat by my side, praying and waiting and patiently answering the questions that I asked over and over again. This was certainly not the first time she'd hovered beside my hospital bed, asking the Lord to heal her husband. God had spared my life many times, and she had to believe he would do it again.

To everyone's relief, I returned to normal the next day. I remembered what had happened and was thankful the injuries had not been more serious. Praise God! Despite my accident, I was confident I would get back on those slopes again.

Fort Totten had its own small version of skiing called Skyline Skiway. The children liked to go there whenever we couldn't get away for a big trip. One cold winter afternoon we took the kids out for a few runs. We were at the bottom of the hill watching as they whizzed down one by one.

Rhonda had worn a scarf that morning over her jacket.

Living the Call

As she grabbed the rope lift and began gliding up the mountain, her scarf became entangled in the rope. Corliss watched in horror as our daughter was lifted off her feet and dangled above the ground with the scarf wrapped around her neck!

"Oh, God, please, help her!" Corliss screamed out, clasping her hand to her mouth.

Rhonda kicked her legs and tried to untangle herself as she continued to be strangled by the scarf. At last the scarf unwound, and she landed with a plop in the snow below. Corliss ran up the hill to her side and held her, thanking God that Rhonda had not been strangled to death in the scarf. It looked as though I wasn't the only one God had sent his angels to watch over on the slopes!

Those angels got quite a workout with our adventurous daughter Rhonda. When she turned 16, she got a job at McDonald's in Devil's Lake to earn some extra money. We agreed to let her drive the family car into town for her shifts.

One morning, after working a late shift the night before, Rhonda returned to town to work an early shift at the fast food restaurant. She hadn't slept much the night before, and I knew she'd be tired when she returned home late that morning.

Just before noon, the phone rang at home. Corliss picked it up and heard Rhonda's frightened voice on the other end of the line. "Mom, I just wrecked the car. I ran off the road and hit the approach at Madsen's."

Corliss turned to me in desperation. "Mel, Rhonda just

The Move

had a car accident! We have to go right away!"

I hurriedly searched for my shoes, but Corliss grabbed my hand urgently. "There's no time for shoes, Mel! Rhonda is bleeding!" she cried.

We found our shaking daughter standing by the Volvo two miles from town; we threw our arms around her and asked if she was all right. She had cut her nose on the steering wheel but otherwise appeared to be okay. Yes, she had fallen asleep at the wheel while driving home from her shift at McDonald's and had drifted off the road, flying over an approach. Overwhelmed with relief that she was fine, we drove her home, praising God the whole way for his protection on her life. The car would need thousands of dollars in repairs, but we could not put a price tag on the life of our precious daughter. I was confident God had marked her to do great things, as he kept his watchful hand on her over the years.

Some of our more memorable family experiences were our summer stays at Lakewood Park Bible Camp. This was the place where Corliss and I had made our first little home; it had changed considerably over the years. The grounds now included a brand-new office complex, which I had worked on, and a brand-new cafeteria. I had been working there as night watchman at the time, and one day my superintendent approached me about working at the camp cafeteria.

"You have to help us out there, Mel," he urged me. "We're in desperate need of someone to manage that place."

Living the Call

My mother was a wonderful cook, and I had picked up a thing or two in the kitchen growing up. Managing a cafeteria seemed like an enjoyable job. I could spruce up my culinary skills, earn a little extra money and get our whole family involved in the action.

"I think it's a great idea," Corliss agreed. She had been serving as camp nurse and a camp counselor for several of the camps. "It will be a wonderful way for all of us to get involved there."

Things were a bit chaotic when I first came to the cafeteria. I had to fire several cooks and replace them, but eventually we got into a groove. I got our older kids involved in the kitchen, the girls making salads and the boys washing pots and pans. We learned where to find the best food at the best prices in town and brought it back to the campground to serve the hundreds of people who came and went throughout the summer.

The first Saturday of camp was especially busy. We stocked up all the freezers and coolers the weekend before to make sure we didn't run out of food. Men's breakfasts, women's luncheons and family camps were among the large groups we served. Roast beef, fried chicken and steaming hot cinnamon rolls were some of the most popular menu items. I planned all the meals for the week, trying to select foods that would appeal to a variety of taste buds. Our family bustled around the kitchen, testing out new recipes and serving hot coffee. We were always generous with our portions; no one ever walked away hungry! Instead the people bragged about how wonderful

The Move

the food was, and some said that it was "served with love." It was a wonderful time for us to bond as a family and interact with all the people who came to camp from the North Dakota churches. Many of the Indians from the reservation attended camp as well. Over time, I learned that we'd gained quite a reputation for serving the best meals the campground had ever seen!

Back on the reservation, God continued to work in miraculous ways. People continued to get saved, attend church and give up their old ways of life. Though we had seen many come to the Lord over the years of our ministry, watching someone turn his or her heart over to God remained a thrilling experience. One particular couple, Calvin and Violet, made a special impression. They came to our church with their seven children, aged 14 to newborn. Soon after they began attending, they got saved.

I was thrilled to see God working in the lives of Calvin and Violet. Not long after this they decided they should get married! It was not uncommon for Indians to have several children together without marrying. Many of them only chose to get married once they got saved and understood the value that God puts on two becoming one. Performing Calvin and Violet's wedding would be especially exciting.

So, after our typical church service one Sunday morning, Calvin and Violet came to the front and exchanged their vows. Their children all sat quietly in the front row, smiling in their best Sunday clothes. Then, one by one, I called them up and dedicated the children to the Lord. As I held the newborn baby in my arms and prayed over him, my heart did a dance. *This* was why we had come to the reservation. These were the moments that reminded me what our ministry was truly all about. What an awesome reason to praise God!

Baptisms were another exciting part of our ministry. It was wonderful to see people not only coming to Christ, but choosing to serve him in obedience by partaking in water baptism. One of our adult Sunday school teachers was set in his ways about the issue of baptism.

"I was raised in a Catholic church and baptized as a baby," he told me. "Why do I need to be baptized again?"

"God calls us to be baptized to proclaim our faith to others," I explained to him. I highly respected this man and understood his logic, but I prayed he would come to understand the significance of this important act of faith.

One Sunday, this man came to me, obviously excited. "Mel, I was preparing to teach on the fundamental truths in Sunday school this morning, and I came to the verses about baptism. I realize you are right, and I want to get baptized right away! When are we going to have the next water baptism?"

At our water baptismal service, this friend was among 38 people who came to the lake to get baptized. As he rose from the water, he was filled with the Holy Spirit and began speaking in tongues.

One by one, the other people began speaking in tongues as they came up out of the water after I immersed them, symbolizing their death to self and their new life in Christ. It was a wonderful moment, as we rejoiced in their profession of faith in God and what he was doing in their hearts.

Tent meetings, church picnics and potlucks continued to be some of our very memorable activities during the summer months. Not only did people come to the Lord during these times, but they grew in their relationships with one another and with us. Corliss and I loved throwing hot dogs on the grill after church and socializing with our church friends, both old and new. I always joked to the congregation that if they were to bring a dish for the potluck, it had better not be a pot with the word "luck" written on the bottom! Lack of food, however, never seemed to be a problem at any events our Indian friends showed up to. And Indian fry bread was always on the table at these feeds.

One of my favorite parts of ministry was seeing people raised up to do God's work among his people. One of these special people was Wilfred, my bus driver. For several years, he remained faithful to our church, driving people back and forth to Lakewood Park Campground, events in town and other activities around the reservation. Wilfred was one of the most stoic Indians I'd ever met; he barely cracked a smile at my many jokes. As I grew to know Wilfred, however, I came to believe he was always laughing on the inside. I was thankful for his dedication to his work; he took driving the bus seriously and remained completely dependable over the years. Without Wilfred, many people would not have been able to attend these life-changing events.

As Shawna's high school graduation approached, Corliss and I began praying more seriously about moving on from the reservation. We had fallen in love with the Indians and were excited about the work God had done in our time of ministry. However, it was time to move on. For the past year, we had felt that God was leading us in a different direction. Shawna, however, was very concerned that we stay on the reservation until she completed high school. She had lived here all her life and wanted to graduate with the kids she had grown up with. We honored her request, continuing to seek God for the next phase of our lives.

Both Corliss and I felt strongly that we should move at least 100 miles from the reservation. We loved the people dearly. They had become like family to us during the 20 years we had spent there. But if we were to be effective in another ministry, we needed to focus on that and not be tempted to drive back and forth to the reservation on a regular basis.

In the spring of 1987, I was appointed Coordinator of Indian Missions for the Assemblies of God in North Dakota and South Dakota. It was quite an exciting adventure, as I would be using my firsthand experience with the Indians in a new, practical way.

The goal was to plant churches and spread the gospel to Indians on all the reservations throughout these two states. I felt passionately about the call to the Indians, as I

The Move

had seen God do such a work in the people already.

"I think we should find a town close to an airport," I told Corliss as we continued to pray for direction. "I am going to be doing a lot of traveling with this new position." And so a local airport became another top priority for our pick of towns.

One weekend, we drove to the town of Minot, two hours from Devil's Lake, where we met with the pastor of the local Assemblies of God church. He was a board member of Central Indian Bible College, with which we had been very involved. We discussed our coming aboard at his church, and he wholeheartedly accepted us. Our missions seemed to be aligned; we found we had much in common. I felt a peace in my heart as we prayed together. It looked as though we had settled on a new place to call home!

We did our research on the town of Minot and found it to be a good match for our family. The small town of Surrey just outside of Minot was rated as one of the top school districts in the state. The sports programs at the schools were excellent as well. This was very important to us, as all of our children were now involved in one sport or another. The town was small enough that we wouldn't get lost in the crowd, but big enough that we'd blend right in, too. With the nearby airport in Minot, it seemed to encompass everything we were looking for.

"I guess we just need to start looking for a house to buy," I told Corliss. The North Dakota District of the Assemblies of God had promised to buy our home on the reservation. With that major matter taken care of, we could now focus on finding a new home for our family.

We drove around the town for a few days, looking at various houses. Our budget was $62,000, and we were insistent upon finding something in that price range. We finally settled on a beautiful home that seemed to fit our family well. We made an offer, and escrow started shortly after.

"This is it! We're really moving! Are you excited?" I asked the kids.

They all expressed positive anticipation. Though they had known nothing else than the reservation, they were all very eager for the adventure of moving to a new town. I was thankful that we had raised such resilient children, easily adaptive to various environments. Moving was never easy emotionally, but we hoped the children would see it as a new adventure, an opportunity to make new friends and widen their circle.

The night before the house was to close escrow, I got a phone call. "I'm sorry, but the sellers decided to sell the home to some friends," our realtor told us grimly. "It looks like things won't work out after all."

My heart sank. We had already begun packing, and Corliss had already started planning where the furniture was going to go! How could things have taken a turn like that? "I know you have a reason for this, Lord, even though we cannot see it right now," I prayed. "Please help us to not be too disheartened and to trust that you have an even better home for us somewhere."

The Move

We continued the search for a house, but it became rather difficult to find anything in our price range. "I think we might have to give up looking," I told our realtor with a sigh. "I just don't think we're going to find anything that will work for us."

"There is one more house I'd like to show you," the realtor said. "It's out in the country a bit, but I really think you'll like it."

"Okay, what do we have to lose?" I agreed.

Corliss and I sucked in our breath as we pulled up to the house. Surely this had to be out of our price range! It was absolutely beautiful. Situated on a large piece of land four miles outside of town, the multi-level house was akin to something one might see in a home and garden magazine. A cheery yellow, it boasted brick accents outside and a sprawling deck out back. The kitchen was complete with a breakfast nook, a stunning dining room with a view of the back yard and beautiful drapes covering the window. A separate living room with a bay window and a step-down family room with a beautiful stone fireplace made up the downstairs. At nearly 4,000 square feet, the home would be more than enough space for our large family. It boasted a spacious laundry room and an office in the back for Mel.

"Lord, if you will supply our means, I will stay in this house for as long as we can," Corliss prayed quietly, her eyes wide as we took in every inch of the house.

"The asking price is $87,000," the realtor informed us. "But it's been on the market for a while, so it's worth a shot to make a lower offer."

I shook my head, nearly laughing. "Well, the most we can offer is $62,000. I doubt they can go that low, but we will give it a go," I replied.

We put in an offer that afternoon, but as we drove away, I laughed out loud. Surely the owners were going to think it was a joke when they got the offer! It would take a true miracle for them to accept such a ridiculously low amount.

To my utter amazement, the owners came back shortly after and made a counter offer of $65,800. I was stunned. We agreed to the amount, knowing we'd find a way to come up with the small difference. I was blown away by how God had worked it all out. Once again, he had taken the seemingly impossible situation and made it possible. He was truly a miracle worker and got all the credit for giving us such a beautiful home!

Word spread quickly on the reservation that the Erickson family was leaving. Our good friends Bob and Carol would be taking over our church, but we knew the change would not come without much sadness. The Indians on the reservation had seen our children grow from infants to high schoolers. We had seen their children grow as well. We had prayed together, cried together and praised the Lord together. Twenty years of memories had been made; they would not easily be forgotten. I was certain there would be no easy way to say goodbye.

Because we had accumulated so many things over the years, we decided the best way to condense our "junk" was

The Move

to hold an auction. As we packed up the house, we set aside the things we would not take with us. I contacted an auctioneer, who agreed to hold the auction on the grounds between our house and the church the following week.

"I think you will get at least $2,000 for all this stuff here," he told me.

I looked around and shrugged. "I doubt we'll get that much, but we'll give it our best shot," I said cheerfully.

The day of the big auction, people came from all over to sift through our goods. We sold everything from the tiniest trinket to a garden tractor and pop-up camper. Corliss was rather disappointed to see her well-worn sofa sell for $13, but we were thrilled to see the camper go for $2,500! When at last the auction was done, the auctioneer handed me $12,000! I was astonished. I had never dreamed we'd bring in that much money. Once again, God provided for our needs in an unexpected way.

With her sofa sold for a mere $13, it was time to find a new one. Corliss had had her eye on a beautiful sofa in town for two years. We went into the furniture store to see if it was still there.

"You're in luck," the employee told us when we arrived. "We put that sofa back in the warehouse, but I can still get my hands on it for you, if you like."

"Oh, could you?" Corliss gasped. "I just loved that sofa, and I've thought about it for the past two years!"

We arrived at the furniture warehouse and were astounded to see that the sofa was not only there, but it had been marked down 50 percent! We were able to

Living the Call

purchase it along with a matching chair. It seemed our patience had paid off. What a blessing to see that God cared about the desires of our hearts!

The night before we were to make the big move to Minot, the kids invited their friends over for an all-night slumber party. Several teens showed up to watch movies, play games, eat pizza, giggle and talk together into the wee hours of the morning. It was a bit chaotic, as we had boxes all over the house, but we wanted to make sure they had one last special memory to cherish before leaving.

Early the next morning before the kids' friends all left, we made breakfast for them. Then Corliss and I went outside to meet the men who came to help us load the U-Haul. Corliss slipped away for a moment down into the empty basement, sat down on a box and cried. So many memories had been made in that house. From the many people we had housed to the kids' friends visiting to the shelves of canned fruit in the basement, this house had held more fun and memories than we could have imagined. It was hard for both of us to believe this chapter in our lives was truly coming to an end.

Our church had held an open house for us the previous Sunday from 2 to 5 p.m. We were blown away at the number of people who showed up to bid us farewell. Though our church attendance had averaged 150 people, it seemed as if hundreds showed up that day. Friends from all over the reservation came. As they hugged us one after another and said goodbye, we were reminded of just how special they had all become to us. Corliss and the children

The Move

all cried as they made their rounds. I held it together but had a hunch that my cry was going to come later.

Michael, always the daredevil, insisted on riding his motorcycle behind our U-Haul as we drove out of town the following Monday. Our van and a pickup truck with a trailer followed behind. Our good friend Russell from church drove one of the trucks. We must have looked quite a sight — a caravan of vehicles piled high with stuff, parading down the road!

As I glanced back one last time, my heart twisted in my chest, and the tears finally came in a flood. Twenty years ago, we'd driven up to that little reservation, uncertain as to what God wanted us to do there. I'd spent my first night trying to break apart a midnight fight, then proceeded to ask God if he'd gotten the "right" guy for the job. But I never could have guessed God would have blessed us with so many beautiful friendships, so many good things and so much fruit for our labor on the Fort Totten Indian Reservation. I would not have traded the last 20 years for anything in the world.

Shawna stayed with us in our new home in the country for the summer before leaving for college. She had graduated as valedictorian of her high school class and was eager to embark on her new college career. We had celebrated her high school graduation with a party in the house at Tokio just two weeks before we moved. We were proud of our oldest daughter and her academic achievements.

We decided to take the summer off from all church

commitments except my position as cafeteria manager at Lakewood Park Bible Camp. We made the two-hour trip back and forth between Minot and Devil's Lake many times that summer. The kids were still working with me in the cafeteria, as well as going to the various camps for their age group as campers.

We also used that time to become acclimated to our new home. We were overwhelmed by the space we'd been blessed with. The kids had their own rooms and enjoyed putting their personal touches on them. I tilled up the garden plot in our large back yard. We planted a garden, and Corliss planted flowers in the flowerbeds around the house. I worked on little odds and ends around the house, as well as making sure our huge lawn was mowed. At night, when we were home, we lay in bed and listened to the rustling of the leaves in the tall trees just outside our upstairs bedroom window with a soft breeze blowing in. Country living was settling well with all of us, it seemed.

The first Sunday we attended our new home church, our entire family sat together in one of the pews. I couldn't remember the last time we'd all sat in one pew together; we must have been quite a sight taking up the whole bench! We chose to attend second service but soon learned all the families with teens attended first service. "We'll see how long the Ericksons keep on coming to second service," Pastor Simmons joked as he introduced us to the congregation.

We were so thankful that the people were receptive to us joining the church in Minot. We had been praying and

The Move

specifically felt called to do tent meetings and evangelical outreaches to the other Indian reservations in North and South Dakota. Our long-term desire was to see Indian churches flourish all over the two states. But for now, we were happy just seeing what God did in the short term and having a home church for our family.

Back on the reservation, the Indians had a hard time getting used to their new leadership. I was confident God had anointed the right people for the job, but the change was especially difficult for some who had known only us as their leaders during their time at the church. We continued to pray for the ministry on the Fort Totten Indian Reservation and for the people in the small town of Tokio. I knew God's work was far from over there; he had already done so much. I prayed they would realize that their faith was not dependent on a person or a leader, but on their very own hearts' relationship with God. Eventually, they began returning to the church and investing again, and we praised God.

It is never easy to say goodbye. Leaving the reservation was perhaps one of the most difficult things our family ever encountered. We had truly fallen in love with the people, and in turn, they had grown to love us. We had seen God perform miracles in the hearts of those who had once hardened themselves to him. We'd watched babies grow up, children blossom into adults and adults marry and have children of their own. We'd seen the end of the cycle of life as well, as we performed the many funerals for loved ones who grieved their loss. And through it all, God had been faithful. He'd been one step ahead of us, preparing our hearts for the work he had for us in the future, always leading the way.

Now, a new chapter of our life had begun. Our children were growing older; our oldest was going off to college. As cliché as it sounds, it really did seem like yesterday that we'd brought her home to that tiny little cottage in the campground. Twenty years had indeed gone by in a flash. With a new home, a new town, a new church and a new mission, we could now sit back and wait on the Lord to see what he had in store for us next. Little did we know of some of the exciting adventures that lay ahead of us.

Chapter Three
Itineration

Life marched on after we arrived in Minot. The children were growing up quickly. Our "baby," Lynelle, was now in the sixth grade. Shawna was heading off to Trinity Bible College in the fall, and Rhonda was already talking about attending North Central, our alma mater, the following year. Michael was nearing his senior year of high school, and Ted and Brenda were just behind him. The days of sleepless nights and diaper changes were far behind us, but a new kind of adventure awaited us.

Shawna enjoyed her freshman year at Trinity Bible College. She continued to play basketball and was a good player on her team. She was a cheerleader for the football team, made good grades and thoroughly enjoyed her time at Trinity. When Rhonda went off to North Central Bible College the following year, she, too, joined the basketball team. Both girls had always had an adventurous, athletic spirit, and we were happy to see they hadn't given up what they loved best.

One weekend, we traveled to Minneapolis to watch Trinity Bible College and North Central Bible College — and, of course, Shawna and Rhonda — play against each other in an exciting basketball game. Seeing our daughters compete against each other would give new meaning to the term "sibling rivalry"! As we drove, I joked to Corliss, "Wouldn't that be something if Rhonda passed the ball to Shawna during the game?"

Sure enough, halfway through the game, Rhonda got hold of the ball and did pass it to Shawna. "Oh, no!" we laughed, "how embarrassing!" But it was more funny than embarrassing, and they both kept up their competitive spirit on the court. They had certainly come a long way from shooting hoops on the little cement court in front of our house on the reservation to playing college basketball!

Rhonda went on to be named All American at North Central. Michael, meanwhile, graduated from high school and began talking about going into the military. He had gone on a missions trip to Portugal and had returned home with a newfound adventurous spirit. He was also intrigued by the posters he saw at the mall advertising for Army recruits. "I think that's what I want to do when I finish school," he told us eagerly.

In the fall of 1989, Michael enlisted in the Army. The Gulf War had just begun, and we learned our son would be shipped off to Saudi Arabia. At 18 years old, he still seemed like a child, but it was time to let him go. We prayed God would protect him as he ventured overseas, and he promised to write us letters often.

Michael faithfully sent one letter after another from Saudi Arabia, telling us he missed us and loved us and was doing well. I tried not to think too hard about the fact that he was halfway around the globe. "Lord, please watch over Michael, and bring him home safely," I prayed fervently.

Itineration

One day shortly before Christmas, we received a devastating letter from Michael. He said that his unit was headed to Iraq on a mission to surround the city of Baghdad. "They have told us that we probably won't come home," he wrote at the end. Our hearts sank as we read that last part. There was always a chance the young men might not make it back alive from their missions, but until now, that young man hadn't been our son. The idea of losing Michael, the precious curly-haired little boy who had brought so much joy to our lives since he joined our family, was heartbreaking.

"God, please let Michael come home, and let him live for you," we prayed through our tears. "But if you do take him, please let him be right with you."

That Christmas, Corliss sang in the church choir's musical production. The church was well known for putting on a huge singing Christmas tree every year. About 100 people stood in a man-made tree singing carols as the Christmas story was played out in a pageant on the stage below. Corliss loved singing in the choir, but as the choir was preparing to walk down the aisle into the sanctuary where the light show in the tree that the choir was about to enter had kept the audience spellbound, a lump caught in her throat. She could hardly keep the tears from coming. What if Michael didn't come home?

To our amazement — and perhaps because of a miracle of God — we rejoiced and praised God when we learned that Michael's unit had returned safely. Operation Desert Storm had been a success. Even more exciting,

Living the Call

Michael told us he had had the chance to share the Lord with several of his new friends in the Army. They knew that they could die at any time as Scud missiles flew overhead, and they kept gas masks ready at their sides in case of a nerve gas attack. Family was important to him during this time; Mike wrote us many letters. He returned safely to the States and was stationed in Fort Worth, Texas.

After only a year at North Central, Rhonda returned to Minot and began studying to become a registered nurse. She had been dating a wonderful guy from the church in Minot since her senior year, and shortly after her return, Shane and Rhonda announced their engagement. We were thrilled that Rhonda would be a new bride! Corliss enjoyed helping her pick out flower arrangements and a beautiful dress.

Meanwhile, Shawna and Kal became engaged as well. Both girls wanted to be married in the spring of 1990, which meant we had double wedding expenses! As missionaries, we had always lived month to month, counting on God to provide for our needs. We wanted to give both girls beautiful weddings and prayed that God would allow us to do that.

A wealthy widow from our church came to us one week with a check. "I want you to take this money and use it for your daughters' weddings," she said sweetly. "Two weddings in a row will surely cost you a pretty penny!"

"Thank you so much," we told her gratefully. Once again, God had come through for us! We were able to give

Itineration

both girls the wedding of their dreams. They would both be young brides, Shawna at 20 years old and Rhonda at 19, but I was thankful they had found such godly young men early on in their lives.

That fall, our younger daughter Brenda eloped. We were quite shocked to find out she'd married in secret, but we held a nice reception for her at the church and remained supportive of her and her new husband. The following summer, Ted married as well. I performed his wedding in the fireside room of our church; it was a small but special event. It was hard to believe that in just one year, four of our six children had married! It looked as though our nest was going to be empty just a bit sooner than we'd expected.

Lynelle went on to high school and began playing basketball, following in her sisters' footsteps. She became one of the best players on her team and was written up in the local newspaper, *The Hoopster*, as being one of the most promising athletes in her age group. We enjoyed going to all of her games just as we had with the other children, cheering her on from the sidelines.

Lynelle made about 90 percent of her free throws the first five games of her sophomore year in the fall of 1991. We went to the next game, and as it started, she was fouled and her free throws came up short of the basket. Our friends came to us after the game.

"We noticed Lynelle isn't making baskets like she used to," they said. "What do you think is going on with her?"

Lynelle came home after the game and said she was

feeling so weak in her arms. I watched Lynelle closely during her next game, and sure enough, she began missing nearly every basket she shot. It was puzzling, as she'd never had any trouble making her baskets. We knew that something was wrong.

We took her to the doctor, who gave her steroids for muscular weakness and said she would gain her strength back. That didn't happen, and she continued to get weaker. The school called and said she had fallen at school, and they were concerned that she would get hurt because her arms did not work. We took her to the doctor again, demanding a better explanation. She was hospitalized for further observation.

One evening, I entered Lynelle's hospital room and saw a girl who looked fairly familiar lying in the next bed. I learned the girl was Jen, a senior at Lynelle's high school, who had suffered a severe asthma attack. She had nearly died in the ambulance and had been revived. It broke my heart to see two young girls fighting for their lives in a dismal hospital room.

I stood between the two beds and bowed my head in prayer. "Lord, please heal Jen and Lynelle. Please return their strength, Lord, and touch them with your healing hand."

The next day, I learned that Jen was going to be released from the hospital. Her lungs had completely opened up, and she was as good as new. I was thrilled to hear that God had answered my prayers for her, but at the same time, devastated that he had not answered my

Itineration

prayers for Lynelle. I walked to the end of the hallway and began to get very angry with God. "How unfair can you be?!" I raged at him. "You heal this girl, but my daughter is still lying in that hospital bed sick!" Bitter tears slipped down my cheeks as I shook my fists into the air.

"Miracles are not for the believer, but for the unbeliever," God whispered to my heart.

I nodded through my tears. God was right. Perhaps Jen's parents did not know the Lord and would come to him through this experience. I knew the Lord, and though he had not chosen to heal my daughter just yet, I had to believe that he, in his sovereignty, knew best.

"We will do everything we can to get her the best help," I told Corliss firmly, trying to stay strong. But even as the words left my mouth, I could feel my heart breaking. Lynelle had always held a special place in my heart as the "caboose" of the family. I wanted whatever was attacking my beautiful daughter to go away — now!

Unhappy with the doctors' treatment plan, we sought out a neurologist in Bismarck at the recommendation of my cousin Roger, who is a doctor. We were met with the grim news: Lynelle had a rare virus called Guillain-Barré Syndrome. This terrible virus attacks one's nerves and muscular system, starting in the arms and legs and then moving to the respiratory system. We were not prepared for such a devastating diagnosis. Both Corliss and I were speechless, unable to believe our vibrant, healthy young daughter could be suffering from something so terrible. We learned that with this particular virus, one's white blood cells attack one's own body. Lynelle would need to have her blood changed on a regular basis to prevent the virus from spreading to her respiratory system and potentially becoming fatal. Surely this could not be happening!

Corliss and I went to our knees, going to the Lord in desperate prayer for our daughter. I had endured many medical ailments in my life, some life-threatening, but watching my own daughter suffer was a whole other story. We cried out to God, asking him to heal Lynelle and restore her health completely.

Lynelle began receiving plasma treatments at a hospital in Bismarck and undergoing physical therapy. She became so weak that we had to help her with her everyday chores, including carrying her books, getting dressed and even holding a spoon to eat. It broke our hearts to see a girl who had once been the star of her basketball team now struggling just to lift a hairbrush.

On Christmas Eve, Corliss sat beside Lynelle in her hospital bed, playing a game of Pac Man with her. "God is going to heal you, Lynelle," Corliss assured her. "We have to keep putting our faith in him."

Lynelle kept up a fighter spirit, staying strong even when we felt like we could not go on. After her initial treatments, she began to regain her strength, but then relapsed after a few weeks. This pattern continued for several months, with Lynelle getting better and then relapsing. We continued to take her to doctors, hospitals and physical therapy, praying all the time that God would give us back our little girl.

Lynelle relapsed several more times; she took turns for the worse on Christmas, New Year's, Easter and Mother's Day. It was devastating to go through what should have been a joyous holiday wondering if we'd ever see our daughter walk strong or play sports again. Corliss and I had been tested in our faith many times throughout the years, but this was the ultimate test of faith. I tried not to become bitter, trusting that God, in his perfect timing, would heal my precious daughter.

On their many trips home from Bismarck, Corliss and Lynelle often stopped at Denny's and had a bowl of Wisconsin cheese soup after her plasmapheresis treatments at the clinic. Lynelle regained strength after each of these treatments and weakly lifted her spoon to her mouth as she ate. She continued to keep up her spirits and sported a smile on her face at even her most dreaded and weakest moments.

One time, Lynelle had to undergo a painful spinal tap. Corliss' heart broke as she watched Lynelle endure more pain than any young girl should have to endure, unable to do anything other than pray for her. It was heart wrenching to see her go through nerve conduction studies and a nerve biopsy as the doctors poked needles into her like a science experiment.

"Lord, I feel so helpless," Corliss prayed. "Please help me to give my daughter the emotional and spiritual support she needs. Please, give us both the strength and patience we need to go on."

Living the Call

At last, one of the doctors pulled us into his office. "I need to be frank with you. If your daughter relapses one more time, we need to send her on to the Mayo Clinic in Minnesota."

My heart sank at these words. Lynelle had already been through so much! I didn't want to send her away for more testing and treatment. A sudden determination rose in my chest, and when I got home, Corliss and I hit our knees once again, asking the Lord to please heal our daughter once and for all.

To our utter relief and joy, Lynelle did not relapse this time! She began to grow stronger every day, doing routine things that had once taken all of her strength to complete. And at last, after a long series of treatments, lab tests, medication and physical therapy, nine months after our very painful journey had begun, our daughter was declared fully healed. We praised God for his faithfulness through our trial. It had been one of the most difficult things we'd both endured. Our faith had been tried, but the Lord had sustained us all. God had given us our sweet daughter back! How we praised God for healing her.

The doctor signed off for Lynelle to play basketball again that fall in her junior year. She had put on some weight due to the steroids the doctors had pumped her up on, but she came back to the sport with a fighting spirit, ready to take on the court once again. She also signed up for volleyball and proved to excel at that, too. How wonderful it was to see our daughter running around with a ball in her hand like old times!

Itineration

After we left the reservation, we knew that we needed to raise our own income for my new job as Coordinator of Indian Ministries in North and South Dakota. We spoke with the district Assembly of God headquarters, and they encouraged us to itinerate, going out and raising funds for our ministry by speaking at churches around the country.

With Lynelle still at home, it only made sense that Corliss would stay behind with her while I traveled around. When Lynelle graduated, Corliss would be able to join me on my trips. I began contacting several pastors around the state, setting up times for me to come to their churches and speak. I specifically wanted to share what God had done on the reservation and how he had worked in the lives of the Indian people during our time there. Although we had many supporters around the country, the way of life of the Indian culture was still a mystery to many. My hope was that believers nationwide would come to see the spiritual needs of the people on the Indian reservations right here in the United States as I had.

Itinerating was both an exciting and an exhausting adventure. I flew to several different cities and states, speaking at one church service after another and sharing about our ministry to the Native Americans. During each service, I brought a variety of Indian artifacts with me representing their culture, including beadwork, arrowheads, hammerhead rocks, peace pipes, paintings and some of the beautiful star quilts we had been given. After speaking about our ministry, I gave a 15- to 20-minute sermon challenging the people to reach out to those in need around them and then closed with a word of prayer. Following the service, the church took an offering for our ministry or pledged monthly support, which would keep us going financially.

As I closed the services, I passed out the ABC tracts Corliss and I had been using for years. "I want you to take these now and go out and spread the gospel of Jesus Christ," I encouraged the congregation. "Don't let what you've heard today stop here."

Word spread, and one pastor after another recommended me to another church. A week after a service, another church would call and ask if I could visit theirs, too. I was always happy to oblige if I could. Preaching was a joy for me, and I had many stories to share — which the audience always enjoyed. From Methodist churches to Lutheran churches to Pentecostal churches, I did not want to pass up an opportunity to share the work of the Lord.

As I traveled, my accommodations ranged from luxurious hotels to rustic cabins with questionable plumbing and heating. I was grateful for anything my supporters had to offer, but on more than one occasion, I got a good laugh out of my sleeping situation.

One winter, I was staying in an old building in a room called the Elijah Quarters. There was a huge thunderstorm in the middle of the night, and there had been a leak in the ceiling above my head. At 4 a.m., I jumped out of bed, itching from head to toe. After finding some lighting, I was horrified to see that my entire bed was covered with

Itineration

ants! They had come out of the walls and the insulation in the ceiling. They had worked their way into every crevice of my body and clothes as well. I shuddered while I tried to brush them off the best I could as I made a run for the shower. That was a night I would never forget!

On another occasion, a church put me up at the Abraham Lincoln Hotel. To call it rustic was an understatement. The sheets were very thin and the towels extremely small. I joked to Corliss later on that it was most likely called the Abraham Lincoln Hotel because it had been built during his era!

I came to see traveling as a wonderful opportunity to spread the gospel wherever I went. Many times, I had the chance to share the Lord with people at gas stations, hotels and airports. On one of my plane trips, I happened to be seated next to a very large man. The plane was completely full that day, and as I folded my long legs under my seat, I saw a guy who must have been almost 7 feet tall come striding down the aisle. "Lord, don't let that man sit between me and this guy," I prayed under my breath, half smiling. I could not imagine any way that the three of us large guys could possibly fit in these three compact seats!

Sure enough, God's great sense of humor prevailed. The tall man approached our row and said without a smile, "That's my seat."

I groaned slightly and let him move in. He sat down and spread out the *Wall Street Journal,* his long, lanky arms going from in front of me to in front of the passenger by the window. I was perturbed, to say the least.

Living the Call

I stuck my nose back in my New Testament and prayed we wouldn't hit turbulence and go spilling all over each other!

As the flight came to an end, the man set down his paper and turned to me. "How are your stocks?" he asked me.

I held my New Testament and smiled. "All my stocks are up!" I quipped.

As we landed, I had a chance to share the Lord with this man and lead him to salvation. I learned that he was the uncle of one of my former classmates. What a small world! And what a great, humbling opportunity for God to remind me that sometimes the least likely people were the exact ones he wanted me to reach.

After I had spoken in more than 60 churches in North Dakota, God began opening doors for me to speak on the East Coast.

I reconnected with my friend Terry Wiles, who had gotten a music degree from Trinity Bible College and had spoken at our church in Tokio. He had since moved to Connecticut and had many connections there. Before I knew it, I was traveling to West Virginia to speak there. As word spread, I continued traveling all over the East Coast, sharing the gospel and stories of what God had done in the lives of people during our time on the Indian reservation and also sharing our vision for the future. God proved faithful, providing for us financially each step of the way. It was exciting to step out of my comfort zone and into new states, other denominations of churches and new relationships with people.

Itineration

During one of my seven-week-long trips to Maryland, I connected with a roommate from Bible college who built wooden glider loveseats. In between church services, I helped him build these gliders, which proved to be a lot of fun. At the end of my stay, I was able to bring one of these beautiful pieces of furniture home to Corliss. My wife was working part-time as a nurse, raising Lynelle and caring for the home while I was away for weeks at a time. I was thrilled to be able to present this glider to her just in time for Mother's Day. She was equally thrilled to get it; it was a beautiful addition to the furniture in our house.

While it was often exhausting and difficult to be away from home for such long periods of time, I was thankful for the exciting things taking place at some of the church services I spoke at. During one particular trip back east, I spoke at a Saturday night service and two Sunday morning services at a small church. I was preparing to speak at one more service that Sunday night and was completely drained. I asked the Lord for a second dose of energy to get me through the rest of the evening.

As the congregation began singing, a lady in a wheelchair was escorted in. She sat in the second row of pews in the church and began raising her voice to the Lord. She could not clap or walk, but she was happy to make a joyful noise as she praised from her heart. I felt saddened for her, as I had a hunch that if she could have, she would have been jumping up and down.

"She is going to walk tonight," I felt the Lord telling me.

Living the Call

What? How could that be, Lord? I argued. *I am totally exhausted from my seven weeks on the road. I am going home in the morning. She is wheelchair-bound!* I believed in the God of miracles and had seen many during my time in ministry, but I wasn't so sure about this one. The lady looked completely crippled; how could she just stand up and walk?

We sang another round of choruses, and again I felt the Lord say to me, "She is going to get up and walk."

Again, I argued with him. "I don't have the faith to pray for that, Lord," I told him.

The leaders turned the service over to me. I began preaching, and as I did, 12 to 13 college-aged students strode into the back of the church and sat down. After I finished speaking, I gave an invitation, and every single one of them came forward to accept Christ as their Savior! They knelt down at the front and bowed their heads in prayer, while I praised the Lord for what he had done.

"I know I just got saved, but is it too soon to be filled with the Holy Spirit?" one girl asked me, her eyes eager.

"If you are open to it, God can do it," I replied with a smile.

Within minutes, this precious young girl began speaking in tongues. I thanked the Lord for her life and the lives of all the others who had come to know Christ. Meanwhile, the crippled lady caught my eye, and I felt compelled to tell her.

"The Lord told me that you will walk tonight," I told her, trying to sound as confident as I could.

Itineration

She looked up at me with wide eyes, took my hand, pulled herself up and then ever so slowly began to move one foot. I gasped as she moved the other foot, too. God was healing her, just as he'd said! Over the next 40 minutes, she began to talk clearly, sharing with me what had happened to her. "I drowned in the Atlantic Ocean years ago," she explained. "The paramedics tried to revive me and then rushed me to the hospital, but I was a near vegetable by then. I spent eight years in a nursing home and have never walked since. The Lord told me I would walk again someday, though." Tears filled her eyes as she looked down at her wiggling feet. "This is a true miracle! God is healing me!"

Tears filled my own eyes as I watched her feet sway back and forth in her wheelchair. My faith had been so small, but God had chosen to heal her! Why, oh why, had I doubted him for a second?

Moments later, she stood to her feet, let go of my hand and began to walk down the aisle! I stared after her in amazement, shaking my head. "Thank you, Lord!" I prayed joyfully. "It was not my faith that healed her; I was merely the guy with a word from you. Thank you!"

At another service, I prayed over a man in his late 50s who had terrible knees. At the end of the service, the man proclaimed that his knees were as good as new and began running all over the place! Praise be to God, the great healer!

One church service in Pennsylvania was especially memorable. I rode with the pastor of the church, a man in his late 80s. After I spoke, a man who was a longtime drug addict came forward and accepted Christ, and we prayed over him for deliverance. We laid hands on him and prayed that the Lord would take away his desire to use drugs from that moment on. After we prayed, the man excitedly announced he wanted to end his destructive lifestyle once and for all. God had delivered him from his sin, and he wanted to start afresh!

"If God can deliver a drug addict, surely he can heal my knees!" A man in his mid-60s stood to his feet. He explained that years of climbing up and down into the truck he drove for a living had taken a toll on his knees. We prayed over him, and God delivered him of his ailment!

The former drug addict went to his car and brought back a huge supply of drugs and drug paraphernalia and laid them on the altar. Included in the pile were several kilos of marijuana, crystal meth, cocaine and several pipes. "I don't want to ever see this stuff again!" he proclaimed.

We cheered with him and agreed to take the drugs and destroy them. We put them all into the elderly man's car and decided to purge them when we got back to his house. As we headed down the road, I couldn't help but cringe. The elderly man's reflexes were undoubtedly not what they once were, and he began to swerve a bit all over the road. "Lord, please don't let us get pulled over," I prayed, chuckling nervously under my breath. "That probably wouldn't look too good for a cop to find all these drugs in our car! We'd have a lot of explaining to do!"

Itineration

We made it back to the elderly man's house, where we proceeded to dump all the drugs in a large burlap bag. We then smashed them to pieces with a sledgehammer and left them in the garbage can behind the house. By God's divine power, those drugs would never be used by that man or anyone else ever again. This young man went on to live for the Lord and attended Teen Challenge at Rehrersburg, Pennsylvania.

I continued itinerating for the next several years while we invested much of our time and resources into the lives of young Native American ministers and Indian churches in the upper Midwest. Corliss was able to travel with me to some of the churches all over the country as we shared the work of the Lord and raised funds for projects on the reservations and for our ministry. At each stop, I made sure to include a gospel message and encourage people that even if they did not go into the mission field or onto a reservation, they could still take part in God's work by supporting the ministry in other ways. I also reminded them that they were all missionaries to their communities and that God had a special plan for each of their lives. The many connections I made along the way were priceless; some of these people would become friends for life.

In 1995, Michael got married in a large, beautiful ceremony in Bismarck. With five of our six children married, Corliss and I could now look toward the future and what it might hold. God had done a great work in the last few years of our lives. He had healed our daughter Lynelle, as well as many who sat in the pews of the

Living the Call

churches I spoke at around the country. Many had accepted Christ as their Savior. God had provided for our needs time and time again and protected us, never letting us down. And though there had been tests and trials along the way, we truly had much to be thankful for as we came through victoriously with the Lord's help.

Mel and Corliss

Itineration

Family picture

Grandkids

Living the Call

Lynelle, Shane, Emma and Elly

Mike and kids

Itineration

Ted's family

Shawna, Kalvin, Chase and Christa

Living the Call

Rhonda, Shane, Logan and Jacob

Chapter Four
Outreaches

As seemed to be the theme of our lives, when one adventure ended, another one began. Corliss and I had established relationships with churches all over the country. We had been able to share our passion for reaching the Native Americans on the Indian reservations with thousands of people. Many Indians had come to Christ because believers had shared the good news with them. Exciting things were happening, but there was something even bigger yet to come.

Shortly after I became Indian ministries coordinator, a missions team from Kansas City, Missouri, came to the reservations of North Dakota. This team of young people brought with them an infectious excitement, as well as many props that caught the Indian children's interest. They put on Vacation Bible Schools for them, complete with games, Bible stories, songs and balloon creations. The children laughed with delight and their eyes lit up as the team members handed them swords, dogs and all types of things made out of colorful balloons. We were impressed by their ability to interact so well with the youth.

One afternoon at Lakewood Bible Camp, the team leader, a man named Mark, came running toward me. "Mel! Mel! I've been thinking. You are so involved with the people on the reservation, and I'm here as well. What if we came alongside you and worked together? Do something even bigger together?"

"Wow, you've got a point there," I replied. "Let's pray about it and see where things go." We began praying and brainstorming over the next few weeks. I loved how the team was engaging the youth with new, creative ideas. What if we could train more teams to go out to all the reservations and replicate what they were doing? Surely, with all our church connections, we could garner the interest. Hands-on outreach is one of the most effective ways to grow in one's relationship with Christ. We could bring the youth together into something really exciting!

And so, in 1992, Conquest was birthed. I began contacting churches all over the country, inviting them to take part in this new ministry. Slowly, the applications began to come in for us to process. God was about to blow us away. The first week in June, groups of people from various states, including Florida, Arizona, Wisconsin, Ohio, Texas, Kansas and Iowa, showed up to our first weeklong training camp at Lakewood Park Campground. Most were young people; some were adults ranging in age from 13 to 68. Some groups came with their youth pastors, and some came on their own. Despite differences in church denominations, age, location and life experiences, they all had one thing in common: They were ready to serve the Lord by taking the message of the gospel to the Indian people on the reservations in the upper Midwest area of the United States.

Outreaches

As I'd been praying about developing Conquest, I felt that the Lord was asking me to do most of the facilitating for the teams. I was in charge of ordering Bibles, manuals, tracts, t-shirts for the team members, balloons and other materials the teams would need as they went out to the various reservations. My job also entailed planning for and getting all the food lined up for the teams in their various places of ministry. Generally a team was made up of 12 to 15 members with 10 or 12 teams going out to different locations all at one time.

Going in a new direction was very difficult for me. I enjoyed having my hands in all sorts of things, but leading people to Christ through sharing the gospel had always been my first passion. "I don't know if I can do this," I lamented to Corliss one night when I got home. "This just feels wrong. I am used to being the soul winner."

"Mel," Corliss said calmly, "do you want to be one person reaching souls, or do you want to be multiplied by 100 people reaching souls out there?"

She had a good point, but I still continued to fight my instincts. I went to our pastor, Dave, in Minot and shared with him my same thoughts. "Mel, do you want to be the one reaching souls, or do you want to be multiplied out there?" he asked me gently.

I half chuckled at his reply. *Okay, God, I get it! Use me wherever I go. I am yours.*

Stepping into this role was difficult at first, but it would also be rewarding to see God using many more people to share the good news.

Living the Call

During the week of the training camp at Conquest, I did much of the speaking, sharing about what to expect on the Indian reservations. "Their culture is very different from yours or perhaps any culture you've ever interacted with," I began. "In order to reach the people effectively, you need to know what is acceptable and what is not on their land. For instance, on some reservations, if a man looks a woman in the eye, this means he wants to pursue her." I went on to explain the many cultural aspects of the Indians, drawing on our myriad experiences on the Fort Totten reservation. "The unemployment rate is high on the reservations. Poverty is the norm. And the children often run in the streets until midnight. Probably a little bit different than the neighborhood you live in, right?" The team members nodded, their eyes wide.

We had the team members write out their own testimonies and practice sharing them with one another. Some, we found out, were not even saved when they first came to the training. We had the opportunity to share the gospel with them and make sure they understood how to invite Christ into their hearts. They were excited to accept Jesus Christ as their Savior and then in turn be able to go out and share Christ with others.

One day, while driving, I felt the Lord say to me, "If you don't bathe the outreaches in prayer, it will be an effort in futility. You must bind the enemy." I knew God was right; I needed to go back and encourage the team members to do the same.

"You are going to encounter much spiritual warfare

Outreaches

while you prepare for this outreach," I shared emphatically. "You'll also encounter spiritual warfare once you reach your destination. Satan would like nothing more than to discourage you from doing the work of the Lord. You must be extra vigilant to pray and ask God to bind the enemy and keep him far away. He will be looking for every opportunity to bring you down." I knew all too well how active the enemy was. He had tried many times to snuff out my life, usually during key times in my ministry. But God always prevailed, and prayer was the first place to start when it came to binding Satan.

It was sometimes easy to forget that the enemy was very much alive and at work. One unforgettable incident was a clear reminder that we always needed to stay on guard. A team of teens from Kansas City encountered a terrifying sight. When their bus pulled into the reservation, they spotted dozens of tiny red eyes peering out from the bushes at them. They began to cry out in fear. But as I walked toward them, they saw two men walking behind me. I had come alone, so I could only assure them that these were two angels, sent from God himself.

"We were so scared!" the youth cried out as they shared what they had seen. They began weeping as they then relayed seeing the two angels behind me.

"Those evil eyes were sent to destroy you, but God sent his angels to protect us," I told them. "Don't be afraid. Satan is at work, but God is also at work, and he will prevail."

Living the Call

"Greater is he that is in [us] than he that is in the world" (1 John 4:4).

One of the most fun parts of the week was engaging the teams in something called human videos. We had seen these videos performed at youth conferences and were impressed by the impact they seemed to make on the youth. Groups of people dramatically pantomime motions to music, speaking with their hands, feet and expressions instead of their words. We were at the forefront of this craze; human videos would go on to become very popular nationwide in the 90s.

I enjoyed stepping outside to see the teams working together on their videos on the lawn at the campground. We had decided that each year Conquest would have a different theme. *Jesus loves me, Jesus is a friend for life, healing for the brokenhearted* and *I want to see* were a few themes we incorporated. One of the favorite human videos included a painted chair, which various people would sit on and get stuck to. This "wet paint" represented sin that sticks to us if we do not stay away from it. The teams especially enjoyed practicing this one.

Many wonderful speakers came to share God's word each year with the teams during the week of training. One of the favorites was Dobie Weasel, the young man who had cut his teeth preaching at our church in Fort Totten. He shared the story of David and Goliath, encouraging the teams to be brave as they ventured into a new "land." His preaching was a highlight of the week. The kids earnestly sought God in prayer for strength as they felt weak and afraid without God's help. These were special times! Joel Cornelius, one of the most precious Indian pastors that I've known, who has a very sensitive heart for the things of God, also ministered to our teams.

Kevin and Konrad, both youth pastors from churches in Minot, came to help direct and to share in teaching/ training times. Their contribution in training the youth in Conquest to go out and witness was invaluable and very helpful for us. We appreciated them.

Corliss stayed at the campground during the week, acting as secretary and nurse. Her nursing skills came in handy once again; she was thankful to be used by God in this new adventure. Lynelle joined us at Conquest and enjoyed working with the kids and helping in human videos. She did much of the behind-the-scenes work for the camps. A talented organizer, she created a lot of our artwork for various pamphlets, the original little kids' coloring book and written materials. We were thankful to be working side by side as a family once again.

As the weeklong intense training came to an end, we began seeing exciting things happening. The teams were growing closer with each other and with the Lord. They were anxious to get out onto the field the following week and reach the Indian people. All of them were filled with the Holy Spirit as we prayed over them. Lives were being changed at Lakewood Park Campground, and the best was yet to come!

On Friday we held a commissioning night, where we prayed over the teams as they prepared to leave for their outreaches. One particular man stood in the back of the room, refusing to join the rest of his team up front. "I don't know if I want to go out and do this," he muttered. "Lord, if you are real, please fill me with the Holy Spirit. I need to know that you are real."

Within minutes, that young man began speaking in tongues. We rejoiced with him as he shared his testimony later that night. He would go on to be one of our most effective soul winners in Conquest.

Many logistics went into planning the actual outreaches. We worked with different churches and schools on the reservations in facilitating showers for the kids in those buildings. These churches and Sunday school classrooms served as sleeping quarters for the teams and their chaperones during their weeklong stay. A kitchen and a cook were also needed, as we fed the teams three meals a day. With Conquest funds, I purchased a fleet of five different vans, which we leased out to the teams.

When the big day came, the team members piled their sleeping bags into the vans and headed off to their various destinations. As we neared the reservation we'd been assigned, they felt the same eerie feeling I always felt when I got close to Indian ground. It was a feeling of evil. Satan was working overtime on these reservations, and he certainly didn't want us to come. "Lord, cover us and help us to win lost souls for you," I prayed as the teams went down the road.

The team members leaned forward in their seats, trying to catch a glimpse of the reservation. I knew they

Outreaches

had already formed a picture of it in their heads. Many had expressed nervousness. I prayed that the Lord would give them the boldness that was promised to them after the infilling of the Holy Spirit as recorded in the book of Acts in the Bible. They had already listened to our speakers talk about it. They knew they needed to depend on God and not on their own strength.

After arriving and settling into their place to stay, the team members set out on a prayer walk. I was quite certain they experienced a bit of culture shock during their first couple of days. Many of them had come from affluent areas and had never seen anything like this in their lives. Most of the Indians on the reservations lived in housing projects: rows and rows of small ranch-style government-built houses lining barren dirt roads. There was usually one grocery store, a school, a gas station and a few other facilities in the town. An occasional basketball court or playground made up the rest of the landscape. I remembered my early days on the reservation at Fort Totten; I must have felt similarly in awe.

During the prayer walks, the teams stopped at each house to invite the Indian children to their outreaches. "We're going to have games, balloons and songs at our big rally tomorrow," they told the children excitedly. "We hope you will come out to join the fun!" Many Indians seemed interested, while others were noncommittal. It was hard to tell how many would really come.

To their delight, nearly 200 people showed up at the outreach the next day. The Indian children were excited to receive an animal balloon and play games. The team members presented their human video out on the grass; the children loved it. At the end of that time, the team members had a chance to share the gospel with the children and ask them if they wanted to invite Jesus into their heart. One by one, their hands went up. A team member would go sit with them, explaining the plan of salvation further and then praying with them individually. Praise God!

"I had my first experience leading someone to the Lord!" one boy told me eagerly when he returned to the base that night. "It was awesome! I was kinda nervous, but God gave me the words."

"That's great!" I encouraged him. "There's nothing better than knowing one more soul is going to heaven." I remembered back to my early ministry experiences, when I'd first led people to Christ. I realized these team members were surprised and even shocked by the positive responses they'd received that day. I had to remind them that though we often assume people don't want to hear about God's word, many times the opposite is true. Often, they are starving for it.

The Assemblies of God had produced a book called the *Book of Hope* that included the gospels of Matthew, Mark, Luke and John. Unlike the Bible, it read straight through like a story from beginning to end, without any repetition. Early on, I pledged to give one to every kid in sixth grade and under; we tried our best to accomplish this. The book proved to be a great tool for many children who had made first-time decisions and had never touched a Bible in their lives.

After a child or an adult made a decision for Christ, we did follow-up with the pastor of the local church. We gave him the decision cards with the names of the ones that had accepted Christ on it. We wanted to make sure that these precious new Christians didn't slip through the cracks, that they would begin coming to church, seeking out and learning the things of God. Our time with them was short, but the decisions they'd made would last an eternity.

At the end of the week, the team members were exhausted but exhilarated. They had stepped far out of their comfort zone to reach the hearts of the Indian people and draw them to Christ. They'd endured sleeping on hard floors and participating in nonstop action under the hot sun, but it had all been worth it.

"I gave my telephone number to a little girl. She wants to keep in touch with me when we leave!" one teenage girl told me excitedly.

"Man, I realize I have a lot to be thankful for back home," another teen piped up. "Some of these Indians have so little, and I have so much. I never want to take it for granted again."

"I want to take this experience back to my school," another boy interjected. "I don't want it to end here. I want to lead kids to the Lord at my school, because they need him there just as much as those Indians on the reservation."

"Those are wonderful testimonies from all of you!" I

exclaimed. Clearly, the experiences made a lasting impression on them. After the outreaches, we had a victory rally where the team came together again for a time of debriefing and praising God for what he had done. One weekend, the vans pulled into the parking lot at Lakewood with dozens of hot, sweaty and tired but happy kids hopping out, laughing and excited to share their experiences with each other. The Bible camp happened to be hosting a partners' banquet. People who had supported Lakewood Bible Camp ministries over the years had been invited to this elegant dinner, complete with beautifully decorated tables and delicious food. All of the attendees were dressed in their finest clothes.

The contrast struck me funny as they sat politely at their tables, while hot, sweaty, enthusiastic teenagers piled out coming straight off the mission field. The contrast between the two groups of people was rather amusing. But both giving and going are necessary!

For the next 11 years, we operated the Conquest program successfully. Each winter, we began taking applications for the following summer. I was amazed at how many people from all over the country wanted to participate. As the summer neared, I began to grow more and more excited about what God would do. Conquest was not just about reaching others for Christ but also about changing the lives of those who went to reach them. I rarely met a team member who did not come back from the experience completely changed and pumped up about serving God in his or her own community.

Outreaches

Over the years, we took our outreaches to several states, including North Dakota, South Dakota, Minnesota, Montana, Wisconsin and Wyoming. While most of the Indians were very receptive to our outreaches, not all were happy we had arrived on their territory. One summer, we took a team to a place called East End Estates. We had heard it was a rather dangerous area, and we were careful to warn the team members about what to expect.

On the first day in this area, the team members set out to do their prayer walks, inviting people in the neighborhoods to the big rally the next day. I sensed many of them were especially nervous; I encouraged them to stay together at all times.

At one Indian housing area, there was partying outside the homes as the team members approached — the residents laughed and hollered loudly over their bottles of beer. Not happy that company had arrived, these rowdy folks sicked their German Rottweilers on the team, sending the feisty dogs straight into the path of the innocent teenagers. The dogs snarled at their visitors, drooling and barking so loudly that the teens had to stand their ground and trust in the Lord. The dogs came within about 10 feet of the young people and then turned and headed back to their owners. The owners continued to tell the dogs to go after the teenagers, but the dogs wouldn't go.

The kids from that housing area picked up several stones and threw them at the young people, only to have them fall short. They knew they could throw farther than that, so they threw harder, only to have their stones continue to fall short of their target. We were thankful God was protecting the team members; no one was hurt.

Two nights later, we learned there had been a murder in that housing tract. The team members were a bit shaken up. The people from the housing tract asked for the young people that had been there a couple nights before. They had the opportunity to speak and minister at the wake in the housing area, and many people came to Christ. They were beginning to get a taste of some of the evil that prevailed on many of the reservations, but also some of the joy and victories of sharing Jesus Christ in the face of evil.

On another outreach, we stayed in a particularly bad area of town. We learned that across the street from where we were staying, drug dealers passed their goods back and forth at a little restaurant. We warned the kids to stay away from that area in case there was trouble. Sure enough, a couple of nights after we arrived, police cars roared up to the restaurant, their sirens screaming. The kids looked on from the church porch across the street in awe as the police drew their guns and frisked the suspects. For many of them, this was putting "getting out of their comfort zone" on a whole other level!

We had the pleasure of returning to Fort Totten to do an outreach one summer. I saw many familiar faces; being there always brought a certain sense of nostalgia. I was anxious to show the kids where our own kids had spent their childhood. Some things had changed on the

Outreaches

reservation, but much of it looked exactly the same. It was hard to believe we had spent 20 years there.

On the last night of the outreach, we held a huge hot dog feed. Hundreds of eager, hungry adults and teenagers showed up, ready to eat. It seemed the line was endless. I began to worry that we might run out of food. To my relief, we never ran out. What a joy to have enough food for everyone!

God was so faithful to us during these years of doing Conquest. He continually met our needs, and he always showed up in a big way at the outreaches. Many times, dark rain clouds crept in just as we were to begin our big rally. We prayed those rain clouds away, and minutes later, the sun would begin to shine! Satan was still trying his best to rain on our parade, but we served a God who was bigger.

Though I had taken the facilitator's seat during Conquest in the soul-winning department, I made sure to never let an opportunity pass me by when I traveled. God brought one divine appointment after another in parking lots, gas stations, eateries and other random places. I continued to remind myself that outreaches don't have to take place on the reservation, but can happen anywhere, anytime.

One weekend, I was on my way to Kansas for an outreach and stopped to fill up my Jeep with gas. I was standing on the cement between the pumps and my Jeep, filling the tank. Suddenly, out of nowhere, a car came careening out of the street, ramming right into my Jeep!

Living the Call

To this day, I do not know how I got out of the way. When things came to a halt, I was standing *behind* my car, watching it all! My heart raced as the reality of what could have happened sunk in. Clearly, my angel, who had so faithfully protected me over the years, was on duty again. I thanked the Lord for miraculously saving my life and protecting me from injury. The devil was up to his old tricks again, but he would not win!

Perhaps the most exciting part of Conquest was the evaluation of what took place during those two weeks each summer.

We counted nearly 20,000 first-time decisions for Christ during the 11 years of our Conquest outreaches — this expanded ministry that God had birthed in our hearts. We learned that many team members had received their call into ministry at Conquest and were now leading youth groups and churches of their own. The boy who had vowed to go back to his school and share about the Lord did just that. Though kids teased him at first, they eventually grew curious about the kid who read his Bible at lunch every day. Over the weeks, he was able to lead more than 50 of his peers to Christ! They became part of the youth group at his church.

Conquest was an unforgettable adventure. Corliss, Lynelle and I were blessed tremendously by the years of working with these precious team members.

We saw God bring together people from all races, church denominations, ages and cultures. And most importantly, we saw thousands come to accept Christ as

Outreaches

their Savior. Conquest was more than just a summer camp or an experience; it was a life-changing event for all.

Conquest training and outreach teams

Conquest training and outreach teams

Living the Call

Conquest training and outreach teams

Conquest training and outreach teams

Outreaches

Conquest training and outreach teams

Conquest training and outreach teams

Conquest training and outreach teams

Living the Call

Conquest training and outreach teams

Conquest training and outreach teams

Conquest training and outreach teams

Outreaches

Conquest training and outreach teams

Conquest training and outreach teams

Conquest training and outreach teams

Living the Call

Conquest training and outreach teams

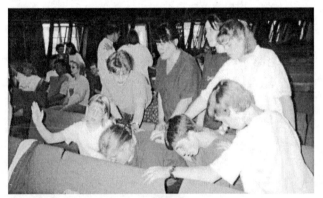

Conquest training and outreach teams

Conquest training and outreach teams

Outreaches

Conquest training and outreach teams

Conquest training and outreach teams

Living the Call

Conquest training and outreach teams

Conquest training and outreach teams

Chapter Five
The Angel

Labor Day weekend, 1991, started out as any other normal holiday weekend. I was managing the cafeteria at Lakewood Park Bible Camp as I had done for the past several summers.

The job was a busy one. From morning till night, I prepared food, planned menus and served three meals a day to large crowds of campers. This particular weekend, I was serving 350 people from Keen Camp, our senior citizens' camp.

On Saturday night, I finished cleaning up a huge mess from the campers and returned to the kitchen around midnight to put out 140 pounds of meat to thaw for the next day. I then trudged back to my motor home to get some rest. My feet ached, and my back was growing sore; I could hardly wait to climb into bed and fall into a deep sleep.

Just a few minutes after I had settled into the motor home, I heard a knock at the door. Surprised that someone was visiting me so late at night, I opened the door hesitantly. A tall, slender man with sandy blond hair and khaki clothing stood before me.

"Can I help you?" I asked him, taking in his unassuming look.

Living the Call

He smiled slightly and stepped inside. He began to tell me all about my life and things that had taken place that I didn't think anyone knew. Who on earth was this guy?

"I know everything about your life, Mel. I was there when the tractor ran you over as a child. I rode with you to the hospital and watched over you as you lay there, fighting for your life. I was there when you went off to Bible college and met your wife. I was there when Corliss crossed the lake that stormy night. I was the one who caused the steering wheel to lock into place so that she would not veer off the bridge. I have been there for each step of your life, Mel, watching over you and protecting you from harm. I am Micah, the big guy who stood behind you in the fight in Tokio."

A lump caught in my throat. "You are?" I whispered, too stunned to say more. My heart began to race. Did this mean he was … an angel? My angel?

I opened my mouth to speak, but no words escaped. I was in complete shock. My guardian angel had a name and was sitting directly across from me in my motor home! It was unbelievable! I stared straight at him, taking in his gentle features and kind smile. As stunned as I was, I had no doubt he had been sent by God with a message for me. And I was ready to sit up and pay attention.

For the next hour and a half, Micah continued to tell me all about my life. He talked in a calm, quiet tone, sharing with me details that only someone who had been right there could possibly know. I remained frozen in my seat, completely mesmerized by his presence. An hour

The Angel

ago, I had been in the cafeteria putting 140 pounds of roast beef in the oven for the noon meal on Sunday, completely exhausted from serving a sit-down banquet for 350 people and cleaning up after they left. But now I was wide awake!

"Mel, the Lord is coming back so soon. You have to be about your Father's business. We as angels will go out and warn people about the Lord's soon return. It is your job to lead them to Christ." As he told of the soon return of Christ and the lateness of the hour, I felt I had a very short time to live.

After he told me all those things, he stood to leave. I stood as well, still at a loss for words. At last, I whispered, "Thank you for coming."

Micah let himself out, and I stood at the door, trying to process what had just taken place. My guardian angel had visited me! I had seen him in person, a man standing before me, a man I could have easily passed by on the street and not glanced at twice. He knew such intimate details about my life that I had no doubt he was sent from God. It was amazing!

After finding my breath, I realized I had so many more questions for him. Would he come back? What else did he know about me or want to say? And why had he chosen me, an ordinary man, to show his face to? On impulse, I raced outside, the door closing behind me as I went out to search for him. It was after midnight and the campground had become quiet for the night, but even in the subtle moonlight, he was nowhere to be seen. I walked up and down the dirt road, hoping to catch a glimpse of my midnight visitor, but he was gone. He had completely vanished.

The oak trees rustled in the cool night breeze as I made my way back to the motor home. It would have been easy to assume I'd imagined the whole experience, that I was simply sleep-deprived and exhausted. But I knew what I had seen and what I had heard. And I was confident it had been real.

Needless to say, I did not get a wink of sleep that night. I tossed and turned, replaying every word of our conversation back in my mind. I wept quietly, asking the Lord over and over, "Why me, God? Why me? No one will believe me when I tell them what has happened!" I waited on the Lord for an answer, but only darkness replied in the stillness of the room.

My thoughts then shifted to death. Perhaps the angel had come because I was going to die soon. Perhaps I had only a few hours left on this earth, and he was trying to warn me about the immanency of sharing the gospel. This idea both frightened and motivated me. If my life here was short, I had to be about my Father's business, as he said. There was no time to waste!

The next morning, I climbed out of bed, exhausted and elated at the same time. The visit with my angel had been surreal, yet I had to go back to my everyday duties in the cafeteria. We had to have breakfast ready for the 300-plus senior citizens who were at the camp. Brother Bakke came through the breakfast line. "I didn't sleep a bit last night," I

The Angel

told him, shaking my head. He did not respond to my not sleeping. I thought about relaying the events of the evening but knew it would sound absolutely ludicrous. For now, I would keep it to myself.

Brother Don was up, telling the campers, "The other night, a young lady picked up a guy halfway between Carrington and Jamestown alongside the road. He rode in silence most of the way and then proceeded to tell her that the Lord was coming very soon. After he got out of her car, she looked back and he was nowhere in sight. This woman was pretty shaken up. I had an opportunity to lead her to Christ. Maybe he was an angel. You never know."

"I do believe there are angels down here on earth, preparing people for the coming of Christ," I replied, my heart racing inside my chest. There was no question in my mind that the hitchhiker was the man who had visited me in my motor home! Goosebumps prickled my arms as I headed off to the cafeteria to prepare the Sunday meals. I had experienced many supernatural things over the years, but nothing could compare to this. How does one carry on with an ordinary day when something so extraordinary has happened to him?

A couple months later, I settled into the sofa in our Minot home on a Sunday afternoon to watch the Vikings play. An avid football fan, I was not about to miss the big game. But as it came on TV, I suddenly felt that the Lord was asking me to go off and pray. I ignored the still small voice and continued watching the game. Again, I felt the nudge to pray, but I chose to brush it off and keep cheering my team on. After the Vikings game ended, I began to watch the Broncos play.

"Don't forget I have to be at the church tonight at 6 o'clock to sing," Corliss reminded me as she popped into the room.

"I won't," I replied, keeping my eyes focused on the TV.

Just before 6 p.m., Corliss and I were headed out the door to church when the telephone rang. I went to answer it and was urgently asked to come over to our neighbor's place. "Elden has collapsed in the yard," the voice on the other end exclaimed. "Can you come right now?"

I dropped everything and raced to our neighbor's place. Elden was lying in a heap on his front lawn, unconscious. I helped carry him inside, and the family and I began performing CPR immediately. I asked, "Have you called 911 for an ambulance?" No one had called yet, so I made the call, gave directions and returned to help with CPR.

Over and over, I pumped the man's chest and breathed into his mouth as I'd learned years before, but my efforts were to no avail. My neighbor remained unconscious; the color began to drain from his face as the minutes ticked by.

Soon the paramedics arrived and took over for us. "It looks like we've got a heartbeat," they shouted as they lifted him onto a stretcher and carried him out to the ambulance.

"Praise the Lord," I whispered. As they closed the

The Angel

ambulance doors, I called out, "I'll stay behind and straighten up!"

In our hurry to try to resuscitate my neighbor, we'd made quite a mess of the living room. I proceeded to push the furniture back into place and tidy up the room and the porch. Suddenly, I looked up and saw a man walk around the side of the house. With only a glance, I knew just who it was.

"If you had gone and prayed instead of watching the game, you could have seen a miracle take place today," the angel said, appearing before me.

I swallowed hard. "No one would have believed it if he'd been raised from the dead," I said hoarsely.

"The miracle was not intended for them. It was intended for you, so that you would know you serve an all-powerful, miracle-working God," Micah told me, his kind eyes piercing mine.

I nodded, speechless once again.

Moments later, Micah disappeared around the side of the house. I raced off to find him, but he was nowhere to be seen. Just like that, he had come and gone.

Later that evening, I learned that my neighbor had passed away in the hospital, despite the doctors' efforts to revive him. I wept, saddened not only at his passing, but at the fact that I had missed out on a chance to see a miracle before my very eyes. He had been in church the previous Sunday, and I was confident that he had a real relationship with the Lord and was now in heaven. Still, I wanted to heed Micah's words. I never again wanted to miss out on a blessing because I did not pray when the Lord nudged.

In October that year, our son Michael called to let us know that his military unit was leaving for Operation Desert Storm in the Middle East. Corliss and I were both disheartened at the news. Michael shared that his commander had informed them that the mission was dangerous; they might never return home to see their families again.

Our daughter Brenda had been away from home at her choice. She was unhappy and going through a period of rebellion. All Corliss and I could do was pray that she would return home safely and give her heart back to the Lord. My heart was heavy for our two children.

One evening that week, I was driving home from a missions service when a phone number popped into my head. I recited these seven digits over and over, confident they were from the Lord. Later that week, the same number came to mind again. On impulse, I picked up the phone and dialed it. To my amazement, our adopted daughter Brenda answered the phone!

"Dad?" Brenda said when she heard my voice on the other line.

"Brenda, please come home," I pleaded. "Your brother is going off to Desert Storm, and this may be the last time we see him. Please, wherever you are, come back to us."

Brenda was quiet for a moment. "Okay," she sighed.

The following weekend, I was due to be at a missions convention in Minneapolis. Corliss and Lynelle were supposed to go with me, but Corliss began to second guess

The Angel

her decision to leave. "I just don't think I should go, Mel," she said, looking obviously torn. "This might be the last time we're all together with Mike. I really think Lynelle and I should stay back at home."

I completely understood and would have loved to stay back to visit with Mike, too, but I had already committed to the convention. With a heavy heart, I headed off to Minneapolis alone.

As my pickup headed down the road, I hardly noticed the changing leaves that danced on the trees and the sun that peeked out from scattered clouds. I began to have a little pity party for myself as I thought about my family back home. I had spent so much time on the road over the past several years, much of it away from the ones I loved the most. I thought this was a chance for my wife and daughter to be traveling with me, and here I was, out on the road by myself.

I stopped at a gas station in Fergus Falls to fill up my truck. As I paid inside at the counter, I saw a man climb into the passenger seat of my vehicle. Taken aback, I turned to the clerk and asked, "Is this common here for people to climb into your vehicle while you're pumping gas?"

The clerk looked confused. "No, sir, I don't think so," she replied, shaking her head.

I walked slowly back to my truck and climbed in. I should not have been surprised to see Micah sitting quietly in the passenger seat. He smiled at me as I closed the door and started the engine.

Living the Call

I fumbled with my seatbelt, stunned that he had come yet a third time to visit me.

Micah wore the same khaki pants and beige shirt he'd worn the previous times. Again, I couldn't help but think how ordinary he looked. Not that I'd expected him to come down in a white robe and a pair of wings with a halo perched atop his head! How many other angels had I passed in my everyday life over the years?

For the next three and a half hours, Micah shared with me more details about my life. I gripped the wheel tightly as I listened to him talk about each of my children by name. He then proceeded to tell me about the day years before when I'd taken a vanload of college students on a road trip and nearly collided with a semi-truck.

"Mel, don't you think God was big enough to lift up that van and set it back down on the road?" he asked calmly.

My heart skipped a beat as I recalled that terrifying day. I'd seen the semi-truck passing another truck and coming directly toward us. I'd been so sure we were going to die. I had closed my eyes and called out for Jesus and was unable to do anything more. When I'd opened my eyes, the semi-trucks were going down the road side by side behind our van, which made absolutely no sense to me. It had crossed my mind that God had lifted our van up, but I'd been too afraid to open my eyes to see. Now the pieces of the puzzle were complete. My God had lifted that van, keeping us out of harm's way. It was a true miracle! I wish to this day that I could have seen the look on the

The Angel

truck driver's face as the van was lifted and set down behind him.

Next, Micah began sharing things about the reservation with me. "Remember the night Tiny was going to kill his wife and you came out to intervene?" he asked. He then went on to describe several more incidents in full detail.

Finally, I found my voice and began asking him questions. My words spilled out on top of each other as they came off my tongue. As I found my words I said, "Micah, when I went off to the fight on the reservation and you showed up behind me, why did the Indians say you were more than 9 feet tall? You don't look to be much more than 6 feet tall right now."

"My size is dependent on the situation," Micah replied matter-of-factly. "I can be whatever size I need to be for the situation I find myself in."

Well, that answered that question! I had replayed that scene many times in my mind over the years. I had had no doubt there had been an angel standing behind me, but now I finally knew who it was. For the first time, I really began to understand what the Bible meant when it says that God knows the number of hairs on your head. God truly cared about every detail of my life and had sent his angel to prove it. How could I ever doubt his love for even a second?

I had so much to learn, so many things to be answered. Micah knew everything about me, yet I knew so little about him. Why had he chosen me? I was intrigued, elated and still a bit shocked that God had sent this angel time and time again to intervene in my life.

"The Lord is coming very soon," Micah repeated. "It's your job to tell the people about him."

The hours passed quickly, and before I knew it, we'd arrived in Minneapolis. As I pulled up to my hotel, I glanced over and saw that Micah was gone. My sunglasses, day planner and half-eaten bag of sunflower seeds sat on the passenger seat just as they had before Micah had climbed in. Like the times before, he'd disappeared just as quickly as he'd appeared. Some might have said I was seeing things, but I knew better. Micah was very real.

The church had put me up in a hotel that night, but after tossing and turning for hours, I concluded they could have saved their money. I was unable to sleep a wink.

In February of the following year, I headed off to Wyoming to speak at a missions convention. When I left Wyoming, I was headed to Kansas City. We were beginning to put the Conquest program together, and I was looking forward to what God was going to do that next summer. Winter was now still at its peak in the area; the temperature gauge on my truck read 25 degrees below zero. I cranked up the heater to keep warm as I navigated the interstate highway in Nebraska.

As I came up to the junction of Interstate 80 and the road that went to Scottsbluff, Nebraska, I noticed I was low on gas, so I pulled off at a truck stop and filled up. As I came to the onramp to get back on Interstate 80, I saw a man standing on the side of the road dressed in khaki

The Angel

pants and a parka. Shocked that he was standing out in such frigid temperatures, I pulled over and let him in.

Within seconds, I had identified the mysterious hitchhiker. He smiled but said nothing as I continued to press my foot on the gas pedal, keeping up my speed of 80 miles per hour.

We sat in silence for some time. At last, Micah spoke up. "If you don't bathe your efforts for your Conquest outreaches in prayer, they will be an effort in futility," he warned me.

I nodded, swallowing hard. I knew Micah had been sent by the Lord with a message for me. Conquest was shaping up to be one of the most exciting things I'd ever done in my years of ministry. But he was right: If I did not bathe it in prayer, it would all be for nothing.

I kept a steady hand on the wheel and didn't slow down at all, but as I looked over to see Micah, he was gone! I had not stopped to let him out. Needless to say, over the next hours it was hard to drive, and tears rolled from my eyes as I sat in the presence of the Almighty God.

In the early 1990s, many Christians began getting caught up in the pro-life movement. Churches gathered together to go out on the streets and protest abortion with signs, shouting out Bible verses and praying for the unborn. While I felt strongly that abortion was wrong, I was not the type of person to go out and march around abortion clinics with picket signs. I began to pray, wondering if I should get out of my comfort zone and join the movement.

Living the Call

As I walked up to my house one afternoon, someone walked in behind me. I spun around and came face to face with Micah once again. This time, instead of his typical khaki attire, he was wearing army fatigues. "The battle is not on the battlefront; it is in the heavenlies," he told me. "The battle is won through prayer and bringing down the strongholds that are in the air. We need to pray for the salvation of those involved in abortion and not go and attack them."

Tears filled my eyes as I took in his words. My angel was right! For years I had preached on the power of prayer and seen it work time and time again. I'd witnessed storm clouds part and the sun come out just minutes before a big event. I'd seen people miraculously healed, seen churches built in weeks when it should have taken months. Only God could get the credit for such amazing events; prayer was truly the answer. Why did we so often complicate things when we had the best weapon of all?

One evening not long after, I got a phone call from a distraught family. "Our daughter is demon-possessed," they explained wearily. "Can you come on Thursday and meet with us to pray for her?"

I remembered Micah's words. "I need to pray and fast first," I told them. "Can we wait a week and then I can come? I don't want to miss out on what our sovereign God can do."

They agreed gratefully. I began praying and fasting, asking the Lord to heal this young girl and bring restoration to her soul and to their home. The following

The Angel

week, as promised, I gathered four ministers from the Minot area and we fasted as a group. We went into the room where the demon-possessed girl was. "In the name of Jesus, be gone!" we commanded the demons.

One by one, the demons screamed as they left her body. We praised God as we saw this once-possessed girl healed before our very eyes. I reminded myself never to go into battle without prayer; it was an essential element to defeat the prince of this world. We prayed the sinner's prayer with the young lady, and she accepted Christ into her life to fill the void where the evil spirits had been. Praise God!

The years passed, and I continued with Conquest and various speaking engagements and work projects. My work took me all over the nation, and it was easy to grow weary from the time spent on the road. One evening, after driving back from South Dakota, I arrived home at 2:30 a.m. and sat down on my front steps. I had logged nearly 60,000 miles on the road that year, and it seemed to be catching up to me. "You can't do this anymore, Mel," I told myself as I put my face into my hands and sighed. "Being away from the family, traveling all over, this is too much." I felt defeated as I took a deep breath and rubbed my aching feet.

Suddenly, Micah was standing before me once again. He sat down beside me and said very calmly and gently, "This battle is not yours, it's the Lord's. He never expected you to win it on your own. He only expected you to be in the battle."

Living the Call

Again, tears filled my eyes as he spoke. Though he had never so much as laid a hand on me, I felt like I'd just received the biggest hug that was humanly possible. God had sent his angel, Micah, not only to exhort me and watch over me, but to comfort me as well. He cared about me, his child, and all the details of my life. Micah was right, as usual. I did not have to fight this battle alone. The Lord only asked me to stand beside him while he did the work.

Micah went on to share more stories with me. He talked about the woman who'd been paralyzed in the church service I'd spoken at, and how, despite my disbelief, God had allowed her to walk. "You were the one chosen to deliver the word of God the night she was healed," he told me.

Chills went up my spine as I recalled that night. I'd had so little faith; I had even told God that I wasn't sure he could heal a woman who'd been wheelchair-bound for so long.

But God had chosen to heal her, and I was able to witness her taking her first steps in years. Despite my unbelief, he had chosen me to be a part of a miracle. I was truly humbled by this.

Another time, Rhonda had gone with some friends to a park one evening. Around midnight, I had an uneasy feeling and drove over to the park several miles away to see what was going on. I stumbled onto a party of teenagers, with my frightened daughter and her friend right in the middle of it. All of a sudden, Rhonda was

The Angel

standing in front of me. "Dad, I knew you were going to come for us!" she'd cried.

As Micah reminded me of this incident, I realized that God had sent his angels that night to surround my daughter until I could reach her. From my tractor accident to my present-day circumstances, Micah had been watching over me. I wondered how many other times I had entertained angels while they walked in my presence!

As usual, Micah disappeared quickly, leaving not a trace of his presence behind. I sat on the steps, the crickets chirping in the background, shaking my head in wonder. I thought back to the first time my angel had visited me in the motor home. I'd been so frightened, so confused. Why had he chosen me, a simple servant of God? Would people think I was crazy if I shared my stories with them? Was I going to die? Those were the thoughts that had run through my mind. But now, I had my answers. Micah had been sent by God to encourage me. Each time, he'd come when I felt I could not go on. He was more than my guardian angel; he was my miracle.

I had recounted the angel visits with Corliss, and then one evening, I sat the kids down and, with great emotion, shared my angel stories with them. They leaned forward, listening intently with wide eyes as I told them about Micah's many visits. I later shared my story in a few church services but decided it wasn't something I wanted to tell everyone. Word of my experiences reached the newspaper, and a reporter contacted me to ask if I'd be willing to share about my special visitor. I declined, however, deciding it was best to keep the stories sacred for the time being.

I have not seen Micah for some time. I like to believe that he still watches over me, that he still rides next to me as I drive down roads of our nation, that I pass him every so often on a snowy afternoon. Perhaps I'll see him again, but perhaps I won't. Only time will tell.

We sing about angels in church, top our Christmas trees with images of them and read about their visitations in the Bible. Yet so often we forget that they still walk among us. They might come in the form of a plain-looking man in a parka alongside the highway or as a visitor in khaki clothing, or we might never know when our paths cross. But one thing is for certain: They are real. How do I know? I know because I've met Micah. And he touched my life forever.

Chapter Six
Church Construction

The decade of the 1990s proved to be a busy time for us. In 1990, Shawna gave birth to little Chase, our first grandchild. We were thrilled at the new addition to our family. A daughter, Christa, was born to Shawna and Kal in 1993. Rhonda and Shane had their first child in 1995, a boy named Logan, while Rhonda was finishing her nurse's training in Aberdeen, South Dakota. Ted and Brenda both had little girls in 1992, Rebecca and Brittney. Michael continued with the military, while Lynelle, our "caboose," graduated from high school and went on to attend North Central Bible College in Minneapolis.

In addition to outreaches, speaking engagements and church building projects, Corliss and I had the privilege of some overseas travel. My father had gotten a refund on airline tickets to Sweden after Operation Desert Storm ended; few people wanted to fly during this precarious time. "You are the only one of the siblings who hasn't been to Sweden before," he told me. "I want you, Corliss and Lynelle to have the tickets and go with us to the home of my birth."

We were thrilled to be able to visit the land of my ancestors (and Corliss' ancestors as well). We spent two and a half weeks enjoying this beautiful country. We picnicked on its rocky shores while the sun sparkled on the beautiful waters of the Baltic Sea. We visited with relatives we had never met and enjoyed their wonderful Swedish hospitality. We visited Stockholm, where we viewed the king's palace and the changing of the guards. We took a train ride across the country, viewing other beautiful cities and green lush countryside in this "Land of the Midnight Sun and Northern Lights."

Following this trip, friends who had been supporters of our ministry invited us to join them as their guests on a weeklong cruise to the Caribbean. It was a wonderful trip as we visited tropical islands during the day and sailed at night. It also set the stage for the next phase of our lives.

On the cruise, our friends introduced Corliss and me to many of their friends from around the country. They came from all denominations, but we all found a common ground: We loved the Lord and wanted to see his work done. We discussed how we could effectively reach people with the good news. When we returned from the cruise, I began to pray about our next mission.

In 1992, I got a call from the pastor of the church on the Turtle Mountain Indian Reservation in Belcourt, North Dakota. "We need help remodeling our church, Mel," he told me. "We are seeing an amazing revival here. People are getting saved, healed and filled with the Holy Spirit. It is an exciting time, but I'm afraid we are running out of room to house our growing congregation."

We contacted people from all over who had expressed interest in our projects, and they offered to help. A group

Church Construction

of people we'd met on the cruise came to assist in the building process, along with a singing group from Pennsylvania. Many had never so much as driven a nail before, but they came with willing hands, and we gladly accepted their help!

The remodeled project only sufficed the congregation for a couple years as they continued to grow. In 1993, the pastor called again, and this time they needed a new church building. "I would be happy to help you," I assured him. I spent the next few weeks drawing up plans for the new church. I was not an architect by any means and had very little experience in construction, but I was confident God would provide me the skills I would need.

When the plans were finished, I took them to a draftsman for a final review. He was impressed by my drawings. A 60x72-foot sanctuary would be located in the middle of the new building. A kitchen, Sunday school rooms and church offices would be on three sides of the sanctuary to complete the 10,000-square-foot structure.

With that detail out of the way, it was now time to work on securing a piece of land. I began praying along with the pastor and his congregation for God's provision. By his grace, we were able to buy 15 acres of land that were not normally available for purchase on the Indian reservation. Even more miraculous, the land cost us only $5,000! Things were really beginning to come along. Praise God!

We had already raised $40,000 for a new building; this was enough to begin the building process. A church member from Walhalla Assembly of God came with his bulldozer and leveled the land so we could begin to build. We had to hire for the footings and the cement slab. We had MAPS teams lined up. The first team, from Oak Grove, Missouri, did the framing of the building. In a week we had the walls up with the windows, doors and roof in place. What a team they were, working 12 to 16 hours a day to accomplish the task.

Fundraising was an ongoing thing. We were thankful for how God was providing. The provider of the materials informed me that we needed to come up with another $10,600 before we could continue building. I went to see an elderly lady in the church who had given faithfully over the years.

"I need to come up with $10,600 to be able to continue to build," I told her. "Is there any way you might be able to help?"

"I can give you the $10,000, but you'll need to come up with the $600," she replied.

"Thank you so much!" I was very grateful for her generosity but got a good chuckle out of her insistence that I raise the other $600. We found a way to raise the money, and we were able to roll forward.

A group of 10 retired RVers joined us as well. They were part of the MAPS, or Mobilization and Placement Services, an organization of the Assemblies of God. They parked their RVs on the church property for the next few weeks; the men helped with construction while the women made pots of coffee and brought snacks to the workers.

Church Construction

They also helped with keeping the building swept and material off the floor. We were so blessed by their presence.

Building was a new adventure for me. I had preached in churches, organized outreaches and ministered to people all over the country, but constructing a church was a whole different ballgame. I learned all sorts of building terms within a short period of time. Within six days, we had the building completely framed and enclosed! The people from the reservation were amazed. We had accomplished so much so fast they had a hard time understanding why other building projects on the reservation were taking so long. They had never seen construction take place so efficiently. I had a hunch it was because we had a "Jewish carpenter" on our side!

Within three months, the entire building was finished. The new sanctuary would now seat 350 to 400 people comfortably. As I walked through the completed rooms, I thanked the Lord for his amazing work. Because of the dedicated work Christian people had done, many more lives would be changed as many more people found the Lord in this church. Even more exciting was the fact that the entire project had cost only $163,000, including the purchase of the land!

The pastor was thrilled with the outcome. Now his growing church would have room to worship and fellowship! "Don't do something too good the first time, or people may want you to do it again," he joked.

I chuckled along with him, but sure enough, word

quickly spread. Soon I was asked to build for other districts that had growing churches on reservations and needed our help. We got a call next from a church in Browning, Montana. They had heard about the beautiful floor plan of the Belcourt church and wanted us to do the same on their property. I agreed to come and began to round up a new team of helpers.

The Montana project was just as successful. Another team from Pennsylvania came and completed most of the electrical work. A team from Sioux City, Iowa, helped do the sheetrock on the new building. And a wonderful man from Buffalo, Missouri, came out to install the heating and air conditioning. It was amazing what could be accomplished when a group of God's skilled and willing workers came together. Again, people were amazed when the new church was finished in less than three months. This was unheard of; most construction projects of this size took almost a year!

While our new adventure was exciting, some sad events took place around this same time. Corliss' mother passed away in 1995, and my father passed away the next year. Corliss' father had passed away several years before; my mother was getting up there in age.

Our parents had played such an integral role in shaping our lives and preparing us for ministry. I had missed having a lot of time with Corliss' wonderful dad. He had been a man who lived close to nature, a peacemaker, a farmer; a man who had etched out the home Corliss grew up in from the land, sawing his own

Church Construction

lumber to build their home and farm buildings. We would miss them all greatly.

After Lynelle graduated from high school in 1994, we found ourselves empty-nested and living in our spacious home out in the country by Surrey with all of our lawnmowers gone and helping hands moved out! So in 1995, we moved from our beautiful home in the country to a condo in Minot, located close to the mall, the church, the airport, the grocery store and the bank. This was a place where the kids loved to stop when they were in town. Ted and Brenda had also blessed us with two more granddaughters, Miranda and Brianca.

In 1996, we had the distinct pleasure of building a new church on our old stomping grounds in Fort Totten. What a sight it was to see all the RV homes of the workers camped in the parking lot of the church while it was being built. And what a lovely location it was with the lake gleaming in the sun only a short distance away and new Indian housing springing up all around.

Meanwhile, I continued to do outreaches during the summers as well. Any extra time was spent with our wonderful grandchildren.

We had enjoyed having barbecues out on the back patio of our home in the country with our married children and little grandchildren, watching them enjoy the big yard in the summer or taking pictures by the fireplace at Christmas time. Now we squeezed them all into our smaller condo for Christmas or birthdays, but enjoyed them just as much. Michael married this same year, 1996, and blessed us with two more grandchildren, Keesha and Trey. God was expanding not only our ministry, but our family as well.

In 1998, God sent us to White Earth, Minnesota, for yet another church building project. This was an especially challenging experience. It rained four or five inches a day while we were there, making it difficult to build. When it came time to pour the cement foundation, huge dark clouds rolled in and hovered directly over our site.

"I think we'd better pray that God moves those clouds on," I announced. The crew pouring the foundation had to leave in the morning, and if it rained, we would not get it done. I went over to the church fellowship meeting area, and we all began to pray those storm clouds away.

Once again, God came through for us. Within minutes, the looming storm clouds began to part, and the sun started to peek its way through. By 4 that afternoon, we had that cement slab finished. We praised the Lord for his perfect timing.

When I first began building churches, I barely had a hammer or saw to my name. Over the years, I accumulated an impressive set of tools to take with me, thanks to the generosity of the volunteers who would buy the tools we needed for the projects. Corliss and I had also been blessed with a new motor home, which we drove and stayed in during these building projects.

Over the weekend, we took a vacation from White Earth for a few days, leaving the motor home behind. The pastor and his wife stayed in the motor home while we were gone. The day after we departed, Pastor Tim phoned us with bad news.

"Someone broke into your motor home last night and vandalized it and stole most of your tools," he said grimly. "My wife and I were called out to minister to a family where a suicide had taken place, and when we returned about 4:30 in the morning, we saw the damage. I'm so sorry."

Things had gone so smoothly thus far, it was easy to forget that Satan was still on the prowl, trying to discourage us from doing God's work. We returned to the site, where the police were investigating the damage. I was saddened to see someone had taken advantage of us while we'd been away.

I called my homeowner's insurance and explained the situation. Fortunately, they covered the tools that had been stolen. We had every brand you could possibly have. The insurance company told us to replace the stolen tools with one brand name instead of trying to replace them with all the original brands. They came and recorded the tools and their serial numbers so if we had anything stolen we could send the information in to them. "Go out and replace all of the tools you had in the tool trailer," the agent instructed me. "We will take care of everything."

The vandals had melted the battery in the motor home and completely shorted out the generator, so the motor home was a total loss. The insurance company paid it off, but we had to stay in motels for the rest of the project.

In September, we started another project on the Pine

Living the Call

Ridge reservation in South Dakota. Over Labor Day weekend we poured the footings and the cement slab, thanks to a group of men from Lead and Rapid City, South Dakota.

While we were pouring the cement in South Dakota, I got another devastating call from the pastor at the White Earth church. "My brother was electrocuted while climbing a pole yesterday," he said sadly. "Can you come and help with his funeral?"

I was distraught at the news. This young man had been the electrician on our project; he was a tremendous help and a wonderful person.

I drove to Minnesota that night and ministered at his funeral. The ceremony was the first service to take place in the new church building. I would rather have come on happier terms, but I was glad I could be of help to these good friends during their loss.

A MAPS team from Oakland, Maryland, came and worked on framing and enclosing the building at Pine Ridge, South Dakota. Another team came from West Virginia and helped finish the outside. They also hung and finished the drywall on the building project in Oglala, South Dakota. I was exhausted when it was completed by the end of the year and said to the Lord, "I will never do two projects in a year again!"

The Lord has a funny sense of humor. After a year off, I took on not one, not two, but three projects! I ventured off to Ballclub, Minnesota, then Poplar, Montana, and then to another church in Montana. It was only by his

Church Construction

strength that I was able to complete them — and only by his grace that I stayed alive!

While I was working on the church parsonage in Ballclub, Minnesota, I had a painful mishap. A board had been placed on the trusses two stories up for us to walk on. As I climbed up on the board to nail something, the board, which was not properly placed on the truss, tipped, and I fell about 8 feet and landed on a second-floor truss, breaking six ribs and one rib in six places. Then, before I knew what was happening, I tumbled onto the floor 8 feet below. In a daze, I got up and went and sat down until I could catch my breath. I continued to work that day and most of the next until we left to return to Minot late that afternoon. Though I was not bleeding, my insides throbbed, and I knew I'd done some damage. I drove our motor home from Minnesota to Devil's Lake and then rode with Brian to Minot. About 30 miles out I told Brian, "I can't take the pain anymore. Get me to the hospital as fast as you can." About midnight I called Corliss and said, "I'm on the way to the hospital. Meet me there." And I hung up.

Sometimes, I guess, a man just doesn't think about all the things he puts his wife through. Corliss didn't know what had happened to me and frantically threw her clothes on and rushed to Trinity Hospital to meet me. "What happened?" Corliss asked as she flew into the hospital room, her face pale as she raced to my side. "Why didn't you call me sooner?"

"I'm fine," I assured her, "just a few internal injuries."

Living the Call

"He broke several ribs and has injuries to some internal organs," the doctor told her. "He's on some pretty strong pain medication right now. He'll need a rest and several days in the hospital."

As everyone knew, it was hard to keep Mel Erickson down for long. I was in the hospital for five days. I needed to take it easy for some time. My friend Bob Few, from out east, became my right-hand man on the project that summer, spending five weeks with me. He insisted I rest and not pick up a thing. I don't know what I would have done without his help — he was a godsend.

Our youngest daughter, Lynelle, graduated from North Central Bible College in Minneapolis in the spring of 1999. In February of 2000, she married the second Shane to come into our family. They blessed us with two granddaughters, Emma and Elly. Emma was born in Phoenix, Arizona, where they lived for five years. Shawna's and Rhonda's families and Corliss and I flew to Phoenix to see that new little addition just before Christmas that year. What a delightful time we all had! Corliss and I made more than one trip to Phoenix for enjoyable visits during that time.

Poplar, Montana, was our last project in the summer of 2000. We started right after the Fourth of July. The MAPS team from Oak Grove, Missouri, helped pour the footing and the cement slab. When the MAPS team from Pennsylvania came to put up the walls, it began to rain heavily. It rained five or six inches on Sunday. We were scheduled to begin putting on trusses at 7 a.m. on Monday morning. I gathered our team of workers, and we began to pray that God would help us get the semi, loaded with the trusses, up to the building, which was surrounded by water and soft muddy soil. The semi came through Poplar at 7 a.m., and the people at the lumber yard started to wager on when we would get them on the building. However, to the astonishment of the people betting that it wouldn't get done, that evening at 6, the semi headed back through Poplar empty! There was a line of cars that came out of town to see what had happened. We had laid planks and the semi had driven up to the building; the trusses were on and most of the sheeting, too!

"You cost us a lot of money down here at the hardware store!" an employee joked to us when we went in for supplies the next morning.

"Why is that?" I asked him.

"Well, we all took bets on if you were going to get them up this week. And we lost!"

"My God is known for coming through like that," I replied with a smile.

Each of the churches we built was based on the floor plans I'd drawn up for the first church in Belcourt. They varied in size from 5,000 to 10,000 square feet, depending on the needs of the congregation. A 50x50-foot sanctuary held roughly 200 people, while a 60x60-foot sanctuary held up to 400 people. Later on, an A-frame building and an eight-sided Indian "Hogan" were among some of our more creative projects. We also built 10 parsonages. Over and over, I acknowledged that it was the Lord, not me, who had orchestrated all the details. I was simply a worker being used by him.

One of the most exciting parts of these building projects was seeing how God provided above and beyond our needs. Many retailers gave us materials at their cost, saving us thousands of dollars. People dropped commercial stoves and refrigerators in our lap on a regular basis. A church provided pews for one of our new churches at no cost to us. Many times, we did not even have to voice our need; things simply showed up.

While working on a church in New Mexico, I got a phone call. "A lighting truck rolled over on the highway," a guy told me. "A man from the area picked up all the lighting and can no longer sell it. He'd like to give you what you can use at no cost."

"We'll take it!" I exclaimed, amazed at how God was taking care of all the details of these churches, from furniture to kitchen appliances to even the lighting!

Part of my job during this time had been to help raise funds for the church buildings. This was quite a big and sometimes challenging responsibility. We had been blessed by the generosity of many supporters over the years. Several of the MAPS RVers had come to us wanting to donate funds. And a few of the churches had already raised a good amount of funds before we began building. I began to pray that the Indians would see the need of accepting more responsibility for raising money for their new church buildings.

The Indians, for the most part, had been very receptive

Church Construction

to the church buildings. Even those who did not attend church seemed supportive and curious. I began speaking in the churches, encouraging the congregations to give to their church building funds. As time went on, they grew excited about doing this. As the walls went up and the insulation went in, they could take pride in knowing that they had helped contribute to their own church building. Seeing them take ownership of these projects was especially meaningful.

Another exciting aspect of these building projects was being able to lead people to the Lord. As I had done my whole life, I tried to look for divine appointments wherever I went. Whether it was at the hardware store or a gas station, I did not want to miss out on any opportunity to lead someone to the Lord. One of the most exciting places we saw lives transformed and people accepting Christ was right there on the building site itself.

At one of our sites, four guys from the reservation came over, looking to help. "We would like to learn all the things that need to be done with building a church," they said eagerly.

I was more than happy to put these four young men to work. But as the days went by, I noticed they had a routine. Before and after and while on breaks from working on the church, they ran off to smoke marijuana and drink a beer. I began to pray that God would work in their hearts and draw them to him.

The last Sunday before the new church was to be completed, the men showed up unexpectedly at the old church building. As the pastor spoke about receiving Christ as Lord and Savior, the men walked forward and made a commitment to Christ. Tears welled in my eyes as I saw them standing at the front of the church, their heads bowed in prayer. This was the reason we had come! A building was just a structure, but a church was a place for sinners to be redeemed. Praise God!

The story didn't end there for these four young men. They went on to start their own drywall business and did quite well for themselves. After completing their first project, they came to the pastor of the church with eager faces. "We got our first check!" they said enthusiastically. "How much do we need to tithe to the church?" The pastor was happy to talk with them. What started as a simple desire to help had led to a life-changing decision!

On three different projects, medicine men came by to see what was happening. When each one came to the building site and into the building, he asked what the presence was that they were feeling. I knew how evil their practices were, and we shared with each of them the message of Christ. By the end of the projects, we were able to lead all three of them to the Lord. One of the men led a march around the church building when it was completed, shouting, "This is God's house. There is no question about it!"

One of both Corliss' and my favorite projects was the church in Wright City, Oklahoma. Not only were the grounds beautiful, lined with the tallest evergreen, oak and aspen trees, but the people were some of the kindest we'd

Church Construction

ever met in our lives. They were desperately in need of a new building. Their sanctuary held only 30 people, and they were growing at a steady pace. People were standing outside around the church during services listening over the PA system.

When I preached in the old sanctuary, the ceiling was only 7 feet high. I am 6 feet tall and felt really tall standing beneath that ceiling. I am also an animated speaker; as I began to preach, I raised my hands above my head and accidentally jammed my fingers into the ceiling! After a good laugh, I confirmed that it was indeed time for a new church building.

All of the people from the church were eager to help build. Pastor Lloyd Lee and his wife prayed fervently for their congregation. Whenever the people came over to the church site, they would pick up a hammer or paintbrush. Some stayed there until 2 a.m. I was impressed at their dedication; this had not been the case with every reservation we'd worked at.

The building was finished in record time in eight weeks. I gathered the congregation and prayed with them over the new church. I asked the Lord to bless it and to bring many new souls to him. I was thrilled to learn that this little church eventually grew from 30 to 80 people. They now also had room for the different age groups of Sunday school classes for the children. God was clearly at work.

Skokomish, Washington, was another one of my favorite projects. Workers traveled all the way from Ohio and Pennsylvania to help build this church. Nestled in the lush Northwest, this reservation was especially beautiful. It rained very hard when we arrived on the site; things became so wet that we actually saw a fish "crossing" the road! We got a good laugh out of that sight.

We happened to be working at the site through the Fourth of July holiday and witnessed a beautiful fireworks display put on by Bill Gates, who owned a home in the area. He set off a spectacular display, but the Indians trumped his with an even more stunning show. We had learned long ago that no one beats the Indians when it comes to fireworks!

In 2005, I traveled to Pinedale, New Mexico, for another building project. We had an especially tough time convincing the Indian tribe there to allow a permit for the water line. At last, we received permission to put it in and were excited to be able to move forward with the project. That day we installed 1,600 feet of water line and got the water to the church.

After a long day's work, we headed into Gallop for a nice steak dinner. It was dark, and I kept my hands firmly on the wheel. As I came up over the hill on the winding rural road, I met several cars, one with its lights on bright. Suddenly I hit something, causing all the airbags in the vehicle to go off. The car was filled with a white fog as I tried to figure out what had happened. My heart raced in my chest as the car came to a quick stop. I had hit something … something big! But what on earth was it?

As I sat there dazed and disoriented, trying to find my

Church Construction

breath, Brian and Pastor Nathan Lynch, who had been following me in their car, came running up from behind to get the car door open and get me out. My thumbs throbbed as airbags had exploded in the steering wheel. "You just hit a horse, Mel!" Brian cried.

A horse?! I was astounded. Having lived in some very rural areas over the years, I had prayed all my life for the Lord to keep animals off the road, especially deer. But I had never made contact while driving with as large an animal as a horse! And in my excitement of finishing such a big part of this project, I had not prayed this time asking the Lord to keep the animals off the road.

I had a serious case of whiplash, but I was thankful that I had no further injuries. The ambulance was called out of Gallop, but I told them to send it back as I was not injured. The horse was lying dead on the side of the road. The rental car was totaled as well. Thank God I was alive! Things could have been much worse — even if I did have to go to a chiropractor for several weeks after I got home.

"You were going 60 miles per hour," the policeman said when he came to the scene. "If you had hit the brakes, that horse would have flown right through your windshield instead of over the top of your car, and most likely you would have been killed. We've had seven people killed in the last five years by horses out on these roads. Be careful out there!" I assured him I would and thanked the Lord for his protection. My guardian angel was once again working overtime!

All in all, I coordinated the building of 21 churches for

Living the Call

Indian reservations all over the country. People from 40 different states came at various times to help out. They ranged in age from senior citizens to teens, but all came with a willing heart. We endured treacherous weather and long, tiring days and traveled many miles; but with the Lord's help, the job always got done in record time. More importantly, we saw many lives touched and changed, not only on the job, but in the new church buildings as well.

On the home front, our family kept on growing, too. In 2004, an extra special blessing came along: Rhonda and Shane's second son, Jacob, was born. Rhonda works as a registered nurse in the ER. Shawna graduated from Minot State University in 2004 with a BS in accounting and is a successful businesswoman. Lynelle's second daughter, Elly, was born in 2005.

After all the children married, Corliss and I had a total of 21 grandchildren. Perhaps there will be more ... time will tell. While we prepared ourselves for the empty-nest syndrome, God filled our lives with grandchildren and adventure instead. The new season of our life proved just as exciting as the rest. But there were still more exciting times to come!

Church Construction

Bob and Judy Koscak (President of IMD)

Construction

Living the Call

New church in White Earth, Minnesota

Construction

New church on Fort Totten Indian Reservation

Church Construction

The Hogan

Ceiling of the Hogan

The Hogan

Living the Call

IMD President's home and office

IMD walls going up

Church Construction

MAPS Team

Men at work on new church

Living the Call

New church construction

Pouring cement slab for new church

Church Construction

Selfridge addition

Selfridge teams at work

Living the Call

The new addition

White Earth, Minnesota - new church being built

Church Construction

Church in Couderay, Wisconsin

Chapter Seven
Katrina

The call came from Convoy of Hope from my friend Ray on a Wednesday afternoon. It was the last day of August, 2005. I was on my way to Grand Forks, North Dakota, to kick off a missions convention. "Mel? Can you go down to Mississippi in your motor home and bring a pickup truck, some generators, chainsaws, Gatorade and water? Convoy of Hope is establishing a distribution site at Gautier, Mississippi, and they need help!"

Just a few days before, Corliss and I had watched the TV intently as reporters confirmed a devastating hurricane in the Gulf of Mexico. It was named Hurricane Katrina and was soon deemed to be one of the worst natural disasters the country had seen in decades. My heart went out to the thousands who had lost their homes in the terrible storm and now remained stranded, hungry and helpless. I had prayed for them as I watched from afar but never imagined God might be calling me to be involved.

Now, as I sat in a plush hotel room on my comfortable bed, I wriggled uncomfortably. "Lord, I don't want to go down there," I protested. "I have several other projects that need to be completed. Perhaps you could send someone else?"

Katrina

I began to pray, and as I did, I felt that the Lord very clearly wanted me to go. However, before I would be able to go, I needed to get a few things in order. I was approved by the Assemblies of God U.S. Missions department to go, but I needed to come up with $5,000 to cover my expenses. Secondly, I needed to find a used pickup truck to tow behind me.

"I've been called to go down to Mississippi to help with Hurricane Katrina relief," I told Corliss on the phone. "However, I need to know that God is in this, so I've asked him to provide a pickup truck and the money I need if I'm definitely supposed to go. I won't go in debt to do this."

Instead of heading home on Thursday morning, I headed for Fargo to attend a car auction, where I attempted to bid on several used pickup trucks. Each time, I was outbid. I remained insistent that I would not go over my $1,500 budget. There was another pickup that was to be auctioned off soon. However, I was being called to go to the parking lot. I wondered why as the next pickup would be auctioned off in a few minutes. Not knowing what was going on, I left the auction and headed toward the parking lot.

A man I had never met before approached me. "Excuse me. I'd like you to come and take a look at my pickup truck over here," he said.

I followed him over to his truck. It was a 1994 Ford extended cab pickup, and it was in beautiful condition. I was sure it was way out of my price range. "Will this work for you?" the man asked, patting the vehicle.

Living the Call

My eyes grew wide. "I'm afraid I can't afford that," I replied slowly.

"I didn't ask if you could afford it. I asked if it would work for you," the man returned, smiling.

"Well, in that case, yes, it would work just fine!" I laughed.

"It's yours, then." The man reached in his back pocket and handed me the title and the keys.

I was shocked and remained frozen for a moment, unable to believe what had just happened as I accepted his gift. This man could easily have sold his truck for thousands of dollars. Yet he had chosen to give it to me, a perfect stranger, for nothing at all!

"Thank you so much! I assure you it will be put to good use!"

I called Corliss and shared the good news with her. "You'll never believe what just happened! A man gave me a beautiful truck in perfect condition! He didn't charge me a penny!" I reported excitedly.

"So I guess this means you're going to Mississippi," Corliss replied.

"Well, no, I'm not going yet. I still need $5,000. I'm not going until I have the money to go."

I drove away from Fargo and called up my good friend in Minot. After I had relayed the latest turn of events to him, he replied, "So you're going to Mississippi, aren't you?"

"No, not yet. I'm not going till God provides the money."

Katrina

I arrived back in Minot that evening and continued praying. God had clearly given me that pickup truck; I was confident that if he wanted me to go to the Gulf, somehow we would see the money come in. I asked people at church to pray. God's timing was always best, and he had always been faithful to provide in the past. I would wait on him.

The next morning, my friend Buddy came to my door. "I want you to have this, Mel," he said, handing me an envelope with $921 that he had collected from various people he'd told of the pending trip. I was blown away. Just like that, God had begun to provide.

On Sunday at church, a man came up and gave me $500. On Monday morning, a small church in Minot presented me with a check for $1,100. My friend Ray gave me $400 that afternoon, and on Monday afternoon, my friend Marv walked up and handed me $1,000. Within a matter of days, God provided the amount I needed to set off to the Gulf. I thanked him and shook my head in wonder. Raising the money had seemed like such a lofty goal, but God, with his always-present sense of humor, had clearly shown me it was time to go.

At 6 p.m. that Monday, I set off in the motor home for Mississippi. Corliss had meticulously packed everything I'd need and then some. Included in my goods were 36 rolls of toilet paper and enough blankets and sleeping bags for an army, which rather amused me. She also stuffed the freezer full of food to keep my stomach appeased on the road. I had no idea how long I'd be gone as I headed down the road, but I was certain I was headed for adventure.

Living the Call

I made my first stop in Rugby, North Dakota, at a gas station. Gas was nearly $4 a gallon, and after filling my tank, I was shocked to see the total came to $143! I stepped inside and pulled out my wallet to pay. "Where are you headed in a motor home in North Dakota this time of year?" a man asked me.

"I'm going to Mississippi to work with the Hurricane Katrina relief," I replied.

"Well, your gas is paid for today," the man said, smiling at me. "That's a good thing you're going to do down there."

"Thank you!" I was astounded by his generosity.

As I prepared to leave, another man approached the counter and handed me $300, and the owner of the station gave me $200. I was overwhelmed. Just days ago, I had been questioning God, wondering if I should really embark on this trip. And now he had made it abundantly clear.

I drove on to Fargo to Thorlow Welding where the pickup truck sat waiting to have a hitch put on. My friend Kevin asked if I'd like to go to breakfast with him the next morning, and we set off for a bite to eat. When I returned to the welding shop, I saw a brand new washer and dryer sitting in the back of the pickup. *What are these doing in here?* I wondered, climbing into the back of the truck to inspect the appliances.

"You take them down there to the Gulf and put them to good use," an employee said.

"Wow! Well, how much do I owe you for the

welding?" I asked, pulling out my wallet.

"A handshake," the man replied with a smile. Once again, I was blown away by God's goodness.

"Thank you so much," I said, shaking my head. "I can't tell you how much I appreciate it."

"Some folks called and told me to tell you to stop at Menards. They have some things for you, too," the man added. "It's just right down the street there." Menards was a local lumber, hardware and everything else store; it's like a Home Depot or Lowe's. I hooked the pickup truck onto the motor home and headed over to the store. Several employees came out to meet me. They loaded the pickup with six heavy-duty chainsaws and four 6,500-watt generators!

"I'm sure you'll be able to use these down there," they declared as they helped me hoist them into the truck.

Another call came in on my cell phone. I was told to go to the local Sam's Club warehouse, where more employees came out with several dozen cases of bottled water and Gatorade. I was nearly speechless by now. At this rate, I'd be amazed if I was able to pull the truck! If there had been any doubt in my mind if I should go to the Gulf, it was all erased now.

I continued on my journey toward Mississippi. Just before Sioux City, Iowa, the engine on the motor home began to make a terrible rattling noise. I slowed down a bit, but the noise continued. "Please, Lord, let me make it to Sioux City," I prayed. I knew people there who could most likely help me out.

Living the Call

God was good, and I was able to make it to Sioux City without breaking down. I called up a friend of mine and explained what was going on. He informed me that he knew of a 24-hour mechanic service in town and that they would be able to take a look at the motor home that evening. I drove up to the mechanic's shop and explained that the motor home was making quite a racket. It didn't take long for the mechanics to determine that a bearing had gone out. However, they said they could not get the idler pulley and bearing until morning.

My friend Loren took me out to eat and got me to a motel close to the truck garage. The next morning, they were able to put the new parts on at the garage and assured me it would be as good as new. Loren also informed me that Morningside Assembly of God, his local church, would be paying the bill. I was humbled by their generosity. I had hardly spent a penny on this trip so far, thanks to the many helping hands along the way. While the motor home was being finished up in the shop, Loren and I went out to breakfast. "I think it's great that you're going down to work at the Gulf," he told me enthusiastically. He pulled a wad of $20 bills from his wallet and slid them across the table. "I hope this will help out a bit."I blinked and accepted the gift gratefully. The bills totaled $300; God had provided above and beyond what I had asked for!

By 9:30 a.m., I was back on the road. My next stop was Arnold, Missouri. After a long day of driving, I pulled off Interstate 55 and into the parking lot of a Comfort Inn.

Katrina

My back ached from sitting in the motor home for so long, and I was looking forward to a good night's sleep. "Do you have room for an old man?" I asked the front desk attendant wearily.

He said, "You don't need a room — you have a motor home."

I told him, "There is so much in there I don't have room to sleep." I explained where I was heading in the morning.

"Tell you what. I'll give you a room for $45. How's that sound?" the man replied. "Why don't you pull your motor home around front so I can keep an eye on it during your stay. I'll also call the Arnold Police Department and have them patrol the grounds."

"Thank you. I sure appreciate that," I said. I reached in my wallet to hand over the cash, but the man waved it away.

"Know what? If you're headed down to Mississippi, you don't need to pay me a thing." The man smiled and plunked a room key onto the counter. "Have a good night, sir."

As I trudged up to my room that evening, I shook my head in disbelief. I had known God would come through with the financing for this trip, but I had not been prepared for such generosity from perfect strangers. I hadn't even arrived at the Gulf yet and already I felt like I'd had a memorable adventure!

After a good night's rest, I got back in the motor home and settled in for another full day's drive. By 2:30 p.m., I began to run into traffic. One National Guard convoy after another was heading down the road in front of me, indicating I was getting close to the disaster scene. I had seen clips on the news and had anticipated heavy police activity, but nothing could have prepared me for such a massive caravan.

Suddenly, I had to hit my brakes hard. An elderly lady drove down the onramp at 35 miles per hour. I heard an odd noise behind the motor home. A sign alongside the road read, *Rest Stop: 2 miles.* "Lord, please let me make it to that rest stop," I prayed. I had been hoping not to encounter any more mechanical troubles along the trip, but apparently that wasn't going to be the case. I pulled into the rest area and found that the hitch that had been put on the pickup had broken and bent under the pickup. I found a phone book in the outside phone booth at the rest stop and made a few calls. "The hitch that attaches my pickup truck to my motor home has come loose, and I need it welded on as soon as possible," I explained when an employee at a local welding shop answered.

"Bring it on in, and we'll fix it," he replied and gave me directions. I unhooked it from the motor home and for the first time drove the pickup that had been given to me.

It took only 40 minutes for the man to weld the part back onto the pickup. It was the first time I had to pay for anything, and they charged me $87 for a few minutes of welding. I drove back to the rest area, hooked up the pickup and continued on my miracle trip.

I arrived in Hattiesburg, Mississippi, and had to fill the

Katrina

pickup with gas and fill six 5-gallon gas containers to bring with me. When I went to the window to pay, the attendant informed me they accepted only credit cards. I was dumbfounded; I'd always been able to pay cash! I was relieved that I had a credit card in my wallet and was able to pay.

Once again, I was back on the road. The caravan continued to crawl along before me. For the first time since I'd started off on my journey, things began to feel very surreal. It occurred to me that I had no idea what I was truly stepping into. I had assumed it would be difficult, even heart-wrenching, to see the devastation, but I was not quite prepared for what I saw next.

As I left Hattiesburg, Mississippi, I began to see the full extent of the hurricane's damage. Trees had blown over to the right and the left; debris was scattered all over the side of the road. What had most likely been a scenic view was now nothing but a barren wasteland. My heart grew heavy as I imagined what it must have been like for these poor people to lose their homes, their belongings and their entire lives in this disaster.

At 9:30 that evening, I called Corliss and told her I was encountering sticky humidity unlike anything I'd ever experienced in my life. The temperature gauge inside the motor home read 95 degrees with 95 percent humidity. I felt as if someone had blanketed me with a sweltering layer of cling wrap.

"I'm almost there," I told Corliss when I reached her at home. "You won't believe all the devastation I've already seen. And it's so hot and humid, I'm going to need a shower every 30 minutes if it stays like this!"

A few minutes into our conversation, the cell phone went dead. Disappointed that I could not finish our conversation, I continued on my way with the motor home. Little did I know that after that happened, Corliss called back, and the operator came on stating there was no cell phone service due to Hurricane Katrina! Corliss felt that we would have no further phone contact for six weeks; she was worried that I might miss my turn in the dark and drive right into the ocean, and she cried for two hours.

It was 10:30 that night when I finally located Gautier, Mississippi, and found the Convoy of Hope site that I was assigned to. It was now too dark to see much, but one thing was for certain: It was hot! The humidity had now reached 100 percent, and the heat index was more than 100 degrees. I was thankful for the generator on the motor home to keep the air conditioner going; there would be no way to sleep without that air conditioner keeping the motor home cool!

Two hours after we lost contact, I was able to get cell phone service and called Corliss back. She said, "Mel, I'm so glad to hear your voice!"

"Why?"

"I thought I wouldn't get to talk to you for six weeks because they said phone service was cut off due to the hurricane! I'm so glad you're okay!"

"I will try to call you as often as I can," I assured her.

Katrina

"And I'm fine. I'm going to get to bed here pretty soon."

Corliss sounded relieved as we said goodbye.

The next morning, I woke up at 6:30 and stepped outside. The air was already thick with humidity and scorching hot. I headed over to the Convoy of Hope truck to see where I was going to be assigned. Within minutes, the jeans and the knit shirt I was wearing stuck to my skin. I had a feeling it was going to be a long day. It was the last day I wore jeans and a knit shirt.

"We'd like you to run the Convoy of Hope distribution site," one of the guys told me when I arrived. "We have several stations set up for those who need assistance. At each station, we'll give them different items, such as water, ice, baby supplies, toiletries, food and cleaning supplies. You'll probably have several hundred cars coming through each day. We're going to try our best to make sure we get to all of them."

Convoy of Hope, a national non-profit organization, was set up to deliver basic essentials to disaster scenes. I was impressed with how organized they were. We had a very old forklift that operated on propane, as well as a semi-truck with a reefer cooling unit on it. The ice we would be passing out was stored on this truck. Piles of non-perishable food goods, including freeze-dried meals, canned goods, cereal and powdered milk, were stacked up at the food station. Pampers, formula and baby wipes were set up at the baby station, while bottles of Clorox and other essentials had been arranged at the cleaning supply station. Finally, bags of toothbrushes, shampoo and soap had been pre-packaged at the toiletries station. It was hard to believe we would probably be completely wiped out of these supplies by evening.

By 7:30 a.m., more than 100 cars were lined up. I watched the long line snake through the parking lot, and again my heart grew heavy for their plight. These people had lost everything; they were now completely vulnerable and depending on us to take care of their very basic needs. Old rusty Buicks and newer shiny sedans were among the cars in the line.

Whether the person inside the car had been a wealthy businessman or an impoverished laborer a week ago, it hardly mattered now. They were all in the same boat of desperation.

"Lord, please give me the opportunity to not only serve these people, but to share your love with them as well," I prayed.

Despite the uncomfortable heat, the day went by quickly. I ran back and forth, gathering cleaning supplies and other pre-packaged items. The Convoy of Hope officials instructed us to put the items in the cars rather than have the people come out to get them; this helped avoid potential chaos.

As each car pulled up, I placed the items inside and tried to speak to the people. My goal has always been to make a person smile or laugh to break the ice. I realized we were under very grim circumstances, but nevertheless, I tried to find something witty to say. Most people were very receptive and grateful. I had the chance to pray with many people and even to lead a lot of them to the Lord in the first day.

"I know it feels so difficult right now, but the Lord cares about your life and has a plan for you. He desires to be in a relationship with you so that you can have eternal life with him. Do you know him as your personal Savior today?" If the person was unsure, I used that opportunity to pray the sinner's prayer with them. It was exciting to know that they were driving off with more than just a backseat full of essentials; they were leaving with a newfound hope in Christ.

By the end of the day, we had served more than 4,000 families. The temperature had risen to 107 degrees with 88 percent humidity. My clothes were completely soaked, and the Dr. Scholl's insoles in my shoes did not serve as a gel but burned and blistered my feet. When we started cleaning up at 6:30 that evening, I realized I had not eaten a thing that day and retreated to the motor home for a much-needed bite of food. Along with the endless rolls of toilet paper, Corliss had packed some hot dogs and potato chips. A good old-fashioned hot dog had never tasted so good.

I was so drained, it didn't take much for me to fall asleep that night. When I awoke at 6:30 the next morning, it was already 92 degrees outside.

"Several people need rides to the airport," Kent, from Convoy of Hope, told me. "Can you do that?"

"Sure thing," I said. I left my post in the care of an 18-year-old missionary boy named Luke who had come to help. When I returned from the airport, the line of cars was still stretched for miles down the road as they lined up for distribution sites.

I had an opportunity to pray with more than 200 people that day and lead many more to the Lord. Tears streaked their dirt-stained faces as they held my hand through the car windows. I had never seen such hopelessness replaced by such hope as I did that day.

One morning, one of the fellows strode over to me. "Mel, why don't you go and take a tour of the area? See for yourself the devastation that the hurricane left."

I agreed to go and hopped in the pickup truck. I had seen the blown-down trees and debris covering the barren roads on my way in, but I'd been so preoccupied driving among the convoys, I hadn't seen the bigger picture. It didn't take long for me to get a grasp of the horrific disaster of Hurricane Katrina. Cement slabs alongside the road were the only indication that houses, stores and businesses had once stood there. Everything had been completely wiped out, as though they had never even existed. My heart sank as I drove slowly, trying to imagine what it must have been like to lose everything so quickly.

I drove slowly for three to four miles, taking in the desolate surroundings. Clothing and parts of houses had been pushed up into the few trees still standing. Swimming pools had been completely lifted from the ground, and only huge holes remained. It was like a war zone; everything was destroyed.

Just up ahead I saw a couple seated upon a piece of

cement. They wrapped their arms around each other and stared out at the ocean, looking forlorn and hopeless. Tears filled my eyes as I watched them. I imagined that at one time this cement had held a beautiful ocean-view home and that inside that home there had been much laughter around the kitchen table at night. Then, like a thief who comes without warning, that beautiful ocean had turned into a vicious monster as the hurricane swept away everything that they knew. Now, they simply clung to each other, for they had nothing else. It was a tragic image that would stick with me for the rest of my trip.

I returned to the site, still shocked from what I had seen. Luke left later that day, and a new team of volunteers from Ohio arrived. I had learned that every four or five days a new team would come in; the hope was that the teams would overlap so that we wouldn't be without some experienced help. I had committed to running the Convoy of Hope site for six weeks, which meant I'd be working with all sorts of people over the duration of my stay.

Four semi-truck loads came in the next morning. I put my "farm boy" skills and natural talent of knowing how to get a job done to use in delegating projects, lifting heavy things and knowing which tools to use in different circumstances. I was a long way from North Dakota, stretched far out of my comfort zone, but God knew that there was a job to be done and that I would be able to do it for him.

Sunday morning, we got word that there was a terrible smell beneath some nearby trees. We called the police and the National Guard, and they came out right away. It didn't take long to uncover the bodies of an elderly couple; they were buried beneath the trees and debris. I was saddened to see them pull the couple out of the rubble. Most likely, the victims had tried to stay behind instead of fleeing the disaster scene. Perhaps they hadn't wanted to leave the only home they had known. But the hurricane had taken their lives. The heat was miserable, and the days were long and tiring, but these tragic situations were devastating.

We didn't open until 2 p.m. on Sunday because of the church services being held that morning. By that time, more than 200 cars were lined up through the parking lot. We didn't close until 6:30 that evening. I was amazed at the steady stream of people who needed help; they just kept coming and coming. To my relief, so did the supplies.

The next few days went much like the others. Cars continued to come steadily, and as the day neared its end, we sometimes had to turn people away. The temperature continued to hover around 100 degrees with unbearable humidity, but we managed to keep going on. I drank plenty of water to stay hydrated, but sometimes in my busyness, I forgot to eat until suppertime. I fell into a deep sleep each night in the motor home, exhausted from a full day's work.

God continued to provide not just the necessities, but the tools we needed as well for the teams to take out sheetrock in the destroyed homes. Someone donated seven brand-new chainsaws, which we used to clear out the trees. Someone else donated wheelbarrows, which also came in very handy. But one thing I felt that we needed was a new forklift. I had been operating the existing one for days to unload the trucks and move the pallets of supplies, but it was difficult to maneuver. I began praying about finding a new one.

On Monday morning, after another frustrating bout with the forklift, I made some calls to try to get my hands on a newer one. I finally got hold of a company in North Dakota that agreed to sell me one for $5,700, nearly half the price of what it should cost, and have it sent down to the Gulf. I was grateful but had no idea how I was going to pay for it; I was confident, however, that I would raise the money. God had provided thus far, and I was sure he would do it again.

"Guess what? I just bought us a new forklift," I told the guys back at the site.

"You did what?" they cried. Everyone knew forklifts cost several thousand dollars.

"Don't worry. I am sure God will provide," I assured them.

I called Corliss with the news. She said incredulously, "You did what, Mel? You bought a forklift?! That's crazy! How are you going to pay for it?" Later that night as she went to church, she told some of her friends the events of the day down in Mississippi. "And my husband just bought a forklift! That makes me just a little bit nervous … a forklift!"

Word quickly spread at the Convoy of Hope office in

Living the Call

Springfield, Missouri. It was reported that "that little old missionary from North Dakota" had bought a forklift! My friend Ray at the Convoy of Hope headquarters overheard the news and almost doubled over with laughter. He called me, and we both had a good laugh. "I am sure not little, and I don't consider myself old!" I said. Nevertheless, I was grateful when our supporters helped me raise the money needed for this large purchase. Within a few hours after hearing about the need, the forklift was completely funded. Once again, God had provided.

People donated some interesting things during my stay. One time, an entire semi-truck full of watermelon showed up. Another day, a whole truckload of sweet potatoes arrived. On another occasion, someone dumped a huge pile of clothing on our site in the middle of the night. We had no idea what to do with it and wanted to make sure we sorted it out before chaos ensued.

A team from North Dakota came to work, bringing water and chainsaws with them. They were such a blessing as they went out and cleared lots of debris.

I had met an elderly lady a few days before who was taking care of her elderly brother and sister. She was living in a lean-to and had no way to keep her food cool. We were able to bring her the fridge we had been given and to hook it up to a highline pole for her to use. She was very grateful for our help.

Many people came to help during the first two weeks I was there. My friends Brian and Kevin came down, as well as another friend from Bangor, Pennsylvania. He gave up two weeks of vacation time to help. Brian delivered the forklift I had purchased. What a blessing it was after unloading two semi-trucks box by box in the heat.

Two guys who called themselves Sponge Bob and Square Pants came as well. They were Royal Rangers leaders with the Assemblies of God and were extremely helpful. They left one morning early, and about 7 a.m., I received a call from them and I heard, "You thought you were rid of me, but guess what! Here I am!" As they were eating breakfast, they had overheard the conversation of some fellows from West Virginia who were thinking about going home because of some of the things they had encountered. So the guys said to them, "You need to go work with Mel at the Convoy of Hope site." He gave the phone to one of the men, and soon they were on their way to work with us. They brought an entire semi load full of food, water, clothing and appliances. There were also 13 men from a fire department who had all kinds of equipment. What a blessing they were as they worked for the next week.

The pastor with the group and another guy stayed to help me, while the rest of the team split into three smaller groups to do cleanup of yards, cut trees and remove ruined sheetrock and insulation out of houses. "Do you know of anyone who needs appliances?" they asked me. I told them about the lady we gave the refrigerator to. They proceeded to bring over a semi load of appliances that we were able to give out. What a God-sent blessing!

Each night before bed, I tried to call Corliss to update

her on what was happening. As the days went by, she began to sense heaviness in my voice. I am always known as a jovial, happy-go-lucky person, but Corliss began to hear a different tone in my voice. It was more than just fatigue; it was an overwhelming sadness over the extreme loss the people there had suffered.

"It's heart-wrenching what's going on down here," I told her honestly. "Each day, I deal with hundreds of people who have literally lost everything but the shirts on their backs. Some have nowhere to go. I know we are helping, but at times, I still feel so helpless. I have a home to return to, but they don't."

"I'm proud of you, Mel," Corliss told me. "I miss you terribly and sometimes feel very alone when I can't talk to you, but I'm praying for you and know that God is going to bless your efforts down there."

One evening, I was just getting ready to close down the site when I heard a woman hollering back at the shaded tent area. "I would have been treated better in hell than the way I've been treated here today!" she cried angrily.

My heart sank at her words. I could only imagine her frustration, but it was saddening to hear that she felt the way she did. I began to pray, asking the Lord for an opportunity to reach her if I could.

A couple days later, I was working the site as usual, car after car in line in need of supplies. I walked by the cars telling them that we had a new crew come in and that we would be a little slow and asking them to please have patience with us. I tried to make light conversation and pray with the weary passengers in each car. Most people were receptive and thankful. I was able to at least get a smile out of several of them. Suddenly, I looked up as I heard a loud *rrumm-rrumm* of an engine rumbling ahead.

There was an old gray Firebird in line. As it approached, I noticed the window was rolled down only an inch. A stone-faced man and woman sat inside. They were more than just weary-looking; they looked hardened. I prayed that God would give me the words to reach them.

I went back to them several times, trying to make inroads with them. After several attempts, I peered through the window and grinned. "I bet she's trouble," I joked to the man.

The man slowly cracked a smile. "Yeah, you could say that."

We began conversing, and little by little, they opened up. They picked up their water and ice and then headed toward the hygiene station. Suddenly, the woman hopped out of the car and ran toward the pre-packaged items. She began demanding a certain type of toothbrush and toothpaste, a certain type of hairbrush and a certain type of shampoo.

Mary approached her gently. "I'm sorry, but we can't do that," she told her. "The bags are pre-packaged with random brands of items." Mary turned and looked at the container of 1,200 pre-packaged hygiene packets, and to her amazement, the very next packet lying on top had everything that this lady had asked for!

Before she could barely finish her sentence, the woman

began to jump up and down. "I can't believe it! This kit has all my favorite things!" Tears filled her eyes as she clutched it to her chest. "I haven't washed my hair in a month," she whispered. "I can't believe this!"

Then Mary asked, "Do you like sweet potatoes? We have a whole bin of them over there." She motioned toward the food station.

"Yes!" she and her husband said as they headed that way.

As they were selecting sweet potatoes to take with them, I went over and began to talk with them about the Lord. After just a few minutes, I was able to pray with them. They were ready to repent and ask Christ into their hearts!

As I walked back to the tent, I was told this was the lady who had yelled that she would have been treated better in hell. What a miraculous turn of events! I thanked the Lord that he had answered my prayer, that he had put that hardened woman in my path and softened her heart.

Over the next week, I had an opportunity to pray with 400 people for salvation. One particular couple pulled up just as we had closed the line for the evening. They were obviously weary and in desperate need; I hated to turn them away. I ran back to the tent for more supplies and helped put them into their car. As I did, I shared the Lord with them and asked them about their relationship with him. They were very receptive to the message and wanted to pray with me. While I prayed, the woman leaned up against me. It was a touching moment, as I realized that it was most likely the first time she had had an ounce of hope in weeks.

A few mornings later, I headed into a nearby town for breakfast at a waffle house that was open. As we were leaving, I saw a familiar-looking couple walk into the restaurant. It was the weary couple I'd recently prayed with! They walked over to me, and we began to talk. "Despite what has happened to us, this has been the best week of our entire life," the man told me happily. Pure joy radiated from his voice! I was amazed. Having a newfound relationship with the Lord had completely changed their countenance. God was so good!

Another day, I had the chance to pray with an older woman whose husband had just had heart surgery. She came back two days later and said to me, "My husband and I are not afraid to die anymore." I was so thrilled that they, too, had found hope and were looking forward to eternal life with Christ.

One day, a torrent of rain blew in, followed by 45- to 60-mile-per-hour winds. Most everyone at the site ran for cover, fearing the worst. Was it possible we were being hit by yet another hurricane?

The wind howled as a few of us tried our best to throw a tarp over the trailer before getting inside. As the stinging rain pelted my cheeks, I was surprised by its warmth. It felt like a warm shower and was actually a welcome surprise amidst the unbearable heat. It quickly covered the ground, turning the parking lot into a torrential river. As I was tying down the tarp, I dropped my Leatherman tool.

Living the Call

"Oh, no!" I cried later when I realized I'd lost it. "I'll never see that again!"

"Don't worry. It will turn up," my friend Ken assured me as we ran for shelter.

"Steel doesn't float." Checking the sky, I prayed that whatever was coming our way wouldn't be as disastrous as Hurricane Katrina. These poor people had suffered so much already; could this area really take any more?

We learned that we'd been hit by Hurricane Rita, another hurricane to land on the Gulf Coast. I praised God that it wasn't as powerful as Katrina. The damage was substantial but not nearly as severe. And to my surprise and relief, the next day I discovered my prized tool had only been washed 300 feet down the "stream" and was lying on the pavement right next to the storm drain. I snatched it up and brushed off the debris.

Corliss, meanwhile, had been watching the news anxiously as reporters shared about Hurricane Rita. Her heart sank as she prayed, *Please, Lord, don't let anything happen to Mel. After all the good things he has done for others down at the Gulf, don't let him be washed out into the sea in a second hurricane.* She told me she grew worried when she couldn't make contact with me, and assumed the worst. Needless to say, she was very relieved when we spoke and I assured her I was okay. She was only a little perturbed about my having to tarp things down with the wind blowing 60 miles per hour and not running for cover for myself!

One of the last things I had the chance to do before I

left was to deliver backpacks with Bibles and school supplies to all the local schools. Several teachers had come to us, concerned because school was slated to start in a week and they had no supplies. I made some calls and was able to deliver coloring books, backpacks, paper, pencils and books to the classrooms. More importantly, the American Bible Society also donated Bibles. The Gideons had also come and passed out New Testaments to the cars in line. It was very exciting to know that God's word was being spread in this devastated area.

Before I knew it, my six-week commitment had come to an end. I had endured 16-hour days in sweltering heat, served thousands of needy people and led several hundred to Christ. The experience had been both heart-wrenching and rewarding. I missed Corliss and my home terribly, but a part of me was also going to miss it here.

My friends Steve and Carol, who were part of the MAPS RV program, came on Thursday to take over my post. I had to be back in Cincinnati, Ohio, to preach at a missions convention a few days later. As I prepared to leave, a huge lump formed in my throat. I glanced around as I climbed into the motor home, taking in the hurricane-ridden Gulf for the last time. As I drove away, the tears began to fall. By the time I was back on the highway, I was crying harder than I ever had before when I'd left a place.

The temperature began to drop as I headed toward Ohio. I breathed a sigh of relief, rolling down the windows to take in the cooler air. As I stopped at gas stations and truck stops along the way, I shared the stories of what God

Living the Call

had done down at the Gulf. I did not want to ever forget what I'd experienced.

I had a chance to pass on that trusty pickup truck to another missionary the following summer. It had served me well, but it was now time for someone else to use it for God's glory. As I handed over the keys, I thought back on my adventure with Hurricane Katrina Relief. I'd been so reluctant to go, but God's amazing provision had sustained me the entire way. Though my travels had taken me all over the country over the years, I had a hunch that the events following Katrina would always hold a special place in my heart.

Chapter Eight
Divine Appointments

For as long as I could remember, I had prayed for divine appointments wherever I went. Whether it was at a gas station, a grocery store, an airport, a church event or a neighborhood picnic, I had prayed that God would place people in my life with whom I could share the gospel. I did not want to miss any opportunity to share the good news of Jesus with those who might not know where they were going when they died. God had been faithful to put these people in my life time and time again.

Right after 9/11, one of my favorite places to share the gospel was on an airplane. Sometimes with hours to pass in the air, it was the perfect opportunity to strike up a conversation with my seatmate. On one particular flight to the East Coast, I happened to sit next to a woman from Seattle. We began talking, and I shared with her that I was a Christian. "Ooh, one of mine!" she replied with a smile.

"God has been so faithful to me over the years. I knew he had a plan for me when he spared my life at age 14." I went on to describe my tractor accident and how God had healed me in the hospital. I then continued to share some of the other stories about my life. As I talked, I noticed that the flight attendants and a few passengers had stopped in the aisles and were listening to me. Since I now had a captive audience, I used this chance to give a gospel message and pray the sinner's prayer out loud.

As the plane came in for a landing, several people walked up to me with gratitude in their eyes. "Thank you so much for sharing those stories and praying," they said one by one. "I asked the Lord into my heart today!"

I was thrilled that God had used me on this flight. It would have been easy to just stick my nose in a book or magazine, but I might have missed out on seeing these new friends give their hearts and lives to Jesus. Though we were now back on land, I had a hunch the angels were singing above us.

I was winding up a trip to the East Coast after being gone from home for seven weeks one spring just before Mother's Day. After speaking in Washington, D.C. on Wednesday, I began the long drive home on Thursday. I was exhausted and was looking forward to a good night's sleep after a long day's drive. I had made a reservation at an Econo-Lodge in Wisconsin, but for some odd reason, I made a last-minute turn into the Comfort Inn across the street instead.

When I stepped inside the lobby, I noticed a young couple standing in front of me. They looked nearly as tired as I did. The clerk ran their credit card and then twisted his mouth into a frown. "I'm sorry, but your card is declined," he said apologetically.

Without hesitating, I stepped forward and handed the clerk my credit card. "I want to pay for their room," I said.

The couple looked up at me incredulously. They were

speechless as I smiled at them and headed off to my own room. I slept well and made my way down to the dining room at 7 the next morning. As I sat down for breakfast, I saw the couple I'd helped the night before, eating with their children. The husband rose from his seat and strode over to me. "Sir, what made you want to pay for our room last night?" he asked me quietly.

"I wanted to do it. I serve a loving God who is faithful to provide for me, and I wanted to show that love to you." I went on to share the gospel with this young man.

"Wow, I can't thank you enough. We are headed to a funeral and had gotten that credit card for emergencies only. When we went out for a late bite to eat last night, we tried it again, and it worked just fine." He paused and smiled. "Tell me more about this God you serve."

I talked with him for some time and was able to lead them to the Lord. Later that month, I got a check in the mail from Iowa. It was from the young couple I'd met; they wanted to repay me for the exact amount of the motel room. They wrote a short letter along with the check, asking where they might find a good church in their area. I was so happy to hear they were pursuing a relationship with God! (By the way, I surprised my wife by getting home for Mother's Day and was greeted with tears of delight because she hadn't been expecting me until after Sunday.)

I had no idea why I'd turned into that Comfort Inn that night any more than that couple had any idea why their credit card hadn't worked. But I did know this much:

Living the Call

It was truly a divine appointment, orchestrated by God. There were no such things as coincidences. God was always at work.

When the tragedy of the collapse of the Twin Towers took place on September 11, 2001, I was miles away from home building a church in Montana. Corliss called and gave me a blow-by-blow account of the devastating news, describing how the twin towers in New York City had been hit by planes, first one and then the other. People were scrambling for their lives with the smoke everywhere as the towers crumbled under terrorist attacks; later we learned how thousands of lives had been taken. I had no access to a television to see the tragedy unfold before my eyes, but I could only imagine the horror. I began to pray for our country and the victims' families as I drove home later that week.

I stopped at a gas station on my way home. As I filled my tank, a man pulled up next to me. "Can you believe it?" he said sadly, shaking his head. "Why would these horrible things happen to our country?"

"It is very sad, but God is in control," I replied. "We are living in the last days, and the Bible talks about these terrible things occurring before Christ returns. Someday, I will be in heaven with him, and the things of this earth will pass away." I went over to finish my transaction at the pump, and when I turned back to get in my car, the man was standing next to my door.

"You are so confident about where you are going when you die, but I'm not," the man said quietly.

Divine Appointments

I seized the opportunity to share a full gospel message with him. When I had finished, the man accepted the Lord into his heart. Another soul would now be in heaven someday because of this "chance" meeting God had arranged. I wanted to make sure I never missed an opportunity to share the good news with friends and strangers alike.

In 1995, Corliss and I moved into Minot from our country home. With the children now grown and starting families of their own, we no longer had the need for so much space. We sold our house and found a wonderful condo two blocks from the mall. We had shared many good memories at our country house; our most recent ones had included family barbecues with the kids and grandchildren. But it was now time to make memories in a new place.

Corliss had spent the past few years working at a nursing home and various medical clinics in Minot. In 2004, she learned about a job with Dr. Zakad, who needed a registered nurse to assist him in his practice. Corliss was an LPN, but was accepted for the job. She was excited about working full time in one place.

On her first day, as Dr. Zakad walked into the office, Corliss greeted him pleasantly. "I'm Corliss, and I will be your nurse," she said. They shook hands, and that was the beginning of an amazing professional relationship between a Pentecostal missionary woman and a Muslim doctor from Pakistan! Corliss also firmly believed in divine appointments and was happy God had sent her to work for a man of such opposite faith. She prayed for him every day and began to be amazed at the opportunities that arose to share the gospel of Jesus Christ with him. She remembers the quiet that came into the room the first time she mentioned the name of Jesus!

In between patients, Dr. Zakad would bring up the subject of religion. "So tell me what makes your God different than mine," he started. He began talking about sacrifices and having to eat Kosher meat.

"Well, Jesus was the supreme sacrifice," Corliss replied. "We don't have to sacrifice anything anymore because Jesus paid the price for our sins when he died on the cross."

Dr. Zakad then mentioned Jesus' resurrection. "He didn't really die," he said. "He just went straight up to heaven. And he is going to come back someday as a Muslim!"

Corliss just smiled. "The Bible has all the answers to the truth," she responded. "Jesus did rise from the dead. It is a historical fact. And he is coming back to rule and reign upon this earth for a thousand years before eternity begins. He is the only one who can straighten this world out and the only one who can provide salvation and healing for his people. Because he rose from the dead, we, too, will someday rise to be with him forever if we have given our hearts and lives to him."

These amazing conversations continued unexpectedly on many different topics regarding the teachings of Christianity versus those of Islam. Corliss enjoyed Dr.

Divine Appointments

Zakad's warm and easygoing personality, but even more she enjoyed the opportunities that came her way to share the things of the Lord with him. Some days, Dr. Zakad slipped into his office to pray to his god, Allah, so Corliss would go into a room to pray to Jehovah, the only one true and living God. She asked the Lord to reveal the truth to Dr. Zakad so that he might come into a true and living relationship with Jesus Christ.

One week, Dr. Zakad went out of town. While he was away, his daughter became very ill. Corliss prayed for the little girl, and she soon became well. When Dr. Zakad himself became ill, Corliss prayed for him and asked the Lord to heal him. She hoped one day he would know the true healer as his personal friend and Savior.

We invited Dr. Zakad and his family over for dinner one evening. His wife was a lovely, friendly woman. They had three adorable sons and a daughter. We were invited to their house in return for an interesting meal with various Pakistani dishes when his parents were visiting them from Pakistan.

Before supper the children were playing downstairs and began asking questions about the Bible, so Corliss began sharing Bible stories with them. They listened eagerly as she talked, making comments and asking questions as she went along. How exciting it was to be able to talk freely about the stories of the Bible to these Muslim children!

Not long after that the Zakads asked us to join them in their celebration of Ramadan. We agreed to go; it would be a new experience for us and perhaps another chance to share Jesus with their Muslim family and friends.

We observed as the group of Muslim people knelt on mats on the floor and recited their prayers to Allah, while we prayed silently to the Lord God Jehovah. Following the prayers, we were invited to eat and enjoy the wonderful meal of chicken and many unfamiliar dishes. Everyone was very happy and friendly; I enjoyed talking with the men, while Corliss engaged in conversation with the women and children.

"So, Mel, tell us about your God," one of the men said out of the blue as we sat around the tables afterward.

"My God is the only one who can save us. He sent his son Jesus to die on the cross for our sins so that we could live with him forever in heaven." I continued to share the things of the Lord with the men while they listened with interest.

"Yes, Jesus is one of our prophets," the men replied, nodding their heads.

"Well, he is the son of God," I responded kindly.

The men were very respectful of my differing faith and did not deny or question what I told them. I prayed that they would one day come to know the true God of the Bible, so that they might partake in a heavenly feast that is far more satisfying than Ramadan!

Corliss worked for Dr. Zakad for two years. Though he never admitted to having accepted Jesus as his Savior, we continued to pray for him and his family, knowing we had clearly presented the truth of the gospel.

Divine Appointments

Dr. Zakad had given Corliss a paperback copy of the Koran. This, of course, gave her the opportunity to present him with a Bible. He kept it on his bookshelf, and when he left, he carefully and respectfully packed it up along with the rest of his books.

Meanwhile, an elderly woman moved out of our three-unit condo complex, and a new family moved in. They were Hindu, from Bangladesh, and were friends of Dr. Zakad's family. Mr. Dieu was a sociology professor at Minot State University, and his wife, a very practical woman, was a stay-at-home mom with two young children. We befriended them right away, excited for another opportunity to share God's love with a family of eastern religion.

Mr. Dieu was a wonderful, quirky man. Though obviously brilliant, he had a bit of difficulty when it came to practical things. He came to our door several times, asking me to back his car out of the garage so he wouldn't hit the wall. I was also happy to help when Mr. Dieu got lost driving home from downtown and when he discovered a mysterious rattling noise in his car (which turned out to be a piece of paper stuck to his tire!). We grew to love their family and were thankful for such friendly neighbors.

One afternoon, Mrs. Dieu came running over to our place. "Corliss, please, I need your help! My neighbor lady just called on the phone. She's crying. Something's wrong! Can you help? My husband took our car to work. Can you drive me down to her house?"

Living the Call

"Of course," Corliss answered, grabbing her shoes. The two women drove the few blocks to her neighbor's apartment. Neither of them knew what was going on or what to expect as they pulled into the parking lot. An ambulance, police cars and a rescue squad car lined the street in front of the building. Our neighbor lady jumped out of the car and ran inside. Some people stood on the steps, wondering what was really going on.

Corliss picked up her cell phone and called me. "Mel, what am I supposed to do? There are rescue vehicles all over and people standing around outside. I don't know if I'm supposed to go or stay or what I'm supposed to do."

"Just do whatever you think you are supposed to do," I replied calmly.

So Corliss parked the car and walked up the steps, asking if anyone knew where the excitement was coming from. An elderly lady was walking down the hall, so Corliss followed her. She told Corliss she was like a grandma to the young couple who lived there. She walked into an apartment unit at the end of the hall, and Corliss slipped in behind her. Once inside, Corliss saw a man in his mid-30s lying on the kitchen floor. He lay pale and motionless with paramedics and rescue workers gathered all around him, obviously trying to revive him.

There were people milling about in the rooms, and his wife paced the floor in another room, talking frantically on the phone in a foreign language. Corliss observed the situation and then brought her attention back to the man on the floor. It seemed as though he wasn't breathing at all, and the rescue workers were not working very aggressively. In a loud whisper, she called out the name of Jesus. This man was too young to die! One of the rescue workers kneeling on the floor turned and looked up at her. Then, suddenly, one of the paramedics looked up at the others and said, "I've got a pulse!"

"Oh, thank you, Jesus!" Corliss walked about on the floor, praying out loud in unknown tongues for this young man as they continued to work on him. The paramedics finally lifted him onto a stretcher and carried him downstairs to the waiting ambulance. Slowly, everyone began to follow, including Corliss.

"Oh, Corliss, pray, pray!" Mrs. Dieu called to her tearfully as she left with her friend to follow along after the ambulance.

"I am! I am!" Corliss assured her as the ambulance moved away slowly out of the parking lot with the paramedics still working over their patient inside.

Corliss returned to the house later that evening and saw Mr. Dieu standing outside near his car. "I'm so scared," he admitted, shaking his head. "Our poor friend, what if he dies?"

"God heals," Corliss replied confidently. "That is, Jesus heals! He hears our prayers and has the power and ability to heal us, if we ask. We will keep on praying for your friend."

Over the next few days, we learned that this young man of mid-eastern descent and in his mid-30s was a medical intern in our town. He had collapsed that afternoon for no apparent reason, but doctors soon discovered he had a heart defect undetected since birth. They had to revive him three more times once they reached the hospital, but were finally able to stabilize him and move him out of ICU. It was weeks before he fully recovered. We prayed for him and his family every day. God had been faithful to hear Corliss' desperate prayers in that apartment building, and we gave him the credit for bringing this young man back to life. We prayed that one day these wonderful Hindu people would also be able to give our God the credit.

"It's a mid-a-cal!" our Hindu neighbor rejoiced later when he learned the young man was on his way to a full recovery.

"A mid-a-cal?" Corliss repeated, dumbfounded. Finally, laughing, she understood what he was saying. It was a miracle! "Yes, indeed, it was a miracle!" she replied, laughing happily.

The Dieu family threw a back yard housewarming party not long after they moved in. Among others, the Zakad family came. We were invited and thoroughly enjoyed ourselves. It was an international party: People from Bangladesh, Pakistan, Turkey, India, Iran, Canada and the United States were there. There was every kind of food imaginable and some things we had never seen or tasted before on tables. Corliss and I were the only adults there who were born in the United States. What a wonderful opportunity it was to mix company with such varied cultures and to let our light shine for Jesus.

Divine Appointments

One day, the young Dieu girl came over to sit with Corliss on our front steps. "Guess what?" she said to Corliss excitedly. "I became a Christian! I went to a Bible school club and asked Jesus into my heart!"

"Oh, that's wonderful!" Corliss replied, giving the little girl a hug. How exciting that this young girl, just 10 years old, had accepted Jesus as the one and only true Savior. We prayed that she would grow in her faith, despite her Hindu upbringing, and perhaps even lead her parents to the Lord.

We were very sad when, after two years, the Dieu family moved away. They had a moving sale to get rid of some of their furniture. Corliss was standing outside with the women chatting when a young man walked up. She recognized him as the man she had prayed for after he collapsed.

"Oh! It's good to see you. We sure prayed for you!" she said.

"So you're the reason," he replied, smiling gratefully.

"No, not us," Corliss replied, shaking her head. "The Lord healed you! What a miracle! We are so thankful you are alive."

I was out on the road when the Dieu family got ready to pull out of town with their U-Haul. They called me on my cell phone as I was driving back toward Minot. "Mel, we won't leave until we get to say goodbye to you," they insisted.

"I'll be back in town soon. I'll meet you over at the Wal-Mart," I replied.

Living the Call

We met in the Wal-Mart parking lot and exchanged goodbye hugs. Though it had only been two years, we felt like we had known the Dieu family our whole lives. We would miss them.

I continued to pray for opportunities to witness to our neighbors. It was easy to forget that Minot was just as much a mission field as other parts of the country or the world. I knew there were people in my very own neighborhood, like the Dieu family, who needed to hear about Jesus.

One evening as I sat outside on a lawn chair in front of our house, an elderly man came walking down the street from the Wellington Senior Center just a block away. He hobbled up our driveway. I guessed him to be in his early 90s; he walked hunched over, taking small slow steps as he neared my house.

"Hi there!" I called out with a wave and a smile.

"Hello." The man reached my porch and stopped to chat. We talked for a while, and at the end of our conversation, I was able to lead him to the Lord! What a great reminder that it is never too late to accept the Lord into your heart.

We still hear from the Dieu family every few months and pray for them often. Though our time with them was short, we cherished every bit of it. We are confident God put the Zakad and the Dieu families in our paths for a reason, just as he did the couple at the hotel, the man at the gas station and all the others we had the opportunity to reach.

Divine Appointments

There are no such things as coincidences in my book, only divine appointments, set by the God of the universe. And as long as we are praying for them, I believe many more will come our way.

Chapter Nine
Alaska and Africa

Corliss and I were keeping busy in the next stage of our lives. I was now working full time as Special Projects Coordinator for Intercultural Ministries with the Assemblies of God. It was a fulfilling ministry that kept me active at all times. Corliss remained my faithful partner, sometimes traveling with me to various locations.

In 2008, we got a phone call from our friends Austin and Jennifer. Austin had come to Conquest from Pennsylvania years before and had given his life to the Lord. We visited with Austin and Jennifer at General Council at Orlando, Florida, in 2003. At that time they told us they were going to Alaska as U.S. missionaries after their two-year itineration here in the lower 48. After much prayer, Austin and Jennifer went on to become pastors of a small church in Emmonak, Alaska.

Emmonak was considered to be in the bush country across the sound, south of Nome on the Bering Sea coast. It was a fishing village and was as rural as one could imagine. It was hard for most people to understand why one would want to leave a comfortable life with modern amenities to serve the people in such remote conditions. However, just as I had been called out of my comfort zone to go work with the Indians on the reservations, so Austin and Jennifer had been called to the bush country of Alaska.

"Mel, we need to get our church painted and get some maintenance work done on the buildings up here," Austin told me over the phone. "Would you and Corliss be willing to come and help us?"

I was excited to put it in my schedule to go. "We would love to," I responded. "It sounds like an exciting missions trip!" We laid plans, secured equipment and supplies and put a team of five in place.

Corliss and I had traveled to many states over the years through our ministry, but we'd never been to Alaska. It didn't take much to convince my wife that it would be an unforgettable trip. We checked the weather and discovered it would be cool even in July and August on the sea coast, so we packed the appropriate clothing. We flew out of Minot to Seattle, and from there we caught another flight to Anchorage. It was cool (63 degrees) and misting.

The next day we explored the city and found Anchorage bustling with businesses, modern shops and a tourist center downtown perfect for picking up t-shirts, gifts and some souvenirs. We loved the feel of the city: beautiful big trees, flowers and a certain indefinable "roughness."

That evening after picking up Loren, Craig and DelWayne, who comprised the rest of our team, we went to eat at Gwennie's Old Alaskan Restaurant for supper. The fresh grilled salmon was so good — so pink, so tender and so delightfully flavored. The ribs were good, too!

Living the Call

We knew we were headed for a very different place as we walked to the end of the airport the next morning. The pilot instructed us to watch our step as we climbed into the 14-passenger plane we were to take from Anchorage to Emmonak. I had to duck as I stepped inside the tiny plane and made my way toward a seat in the center. There were just seven single seats on each side of the aircraft and not enough headroom to stand up straight. I sat down gingerly and buckled in, noting the duct tape holding the windows and air exchange in place! "Lord, it's going to be just you and me up there," I prayed, looking across the aisle at Corliss with a slightly nervous grin. "God, please help us get through this flight."

The engine made a loud rattling noise as we took off, and I began to pray harder. It was a very noisy flight, too noisy to talk. However, we did venture to look down at the vast mountain peaks below us and even got a glimpse of the top of Mount McKinley above the clouds. Soon, I felt my heart began to calm and actually fell asleep for a while; but Corliss was still praying, "Oh, God, it's just you and me up here!"

When I awoke, we were flying over the Alaskan tundra, stretching for miles and miles like a rippled blanket. It was undoubtedly nondescript and barren in comparison to the very beautiful area surrounded by mountains that we had just left.

"We're here!" the pilot announced. Corliss and I had never been so happy to put both feet on the ground. We stepped out of the plane and breathed a small sigh of relief and anticipation of what lay ahead. Our missionary friend Austin Jones met us at the tiny airport. He had worked with us on several projects in North Dakota, and we would now be accompanying him to his home to work on his missions projects.

"Go ahead and throw your suitcases in the back," he said after greeting us warmly, pointing toward a wooden-sided trailer pulled by a large ATV four-wheeler.

"So this is our transportation?" I grinned as we loaded our suitcases into the back of the trailer.

"Yes, get in!" he said. I wish you could have seen the look on my wife's face. She just hadn't thought about how we were going to get to our friends' house from the tiny airport just outside of town. "There are no cars in this town," Austin said with a smile, "just ATV four-wheelers!"

It was the end of July, but it was very cool in this little corner of the world. The sky was gray, and a light rain splashed on our faces as we bounced up the dirt road into town in the small wooden trailer pulled by the four-wheeler. We waved at people standing by the road or alongside their dark grey houses or as we met them driving along on their four-wheelers.

In northern Alaska, it is light out 24 hours a day during the summer, while in the winter, the sun doesn't shine at all. I assumed this must be very difficult to get used to. We were such creatures of habit, used to sleeping when the sun went down. *Alaska would prove to be more different than anywhere else we'd ever been,* I mused.

Upon arriving, I was surprised to see flat ground and

virtually no big trees. The brush that was there was perhaps 8 feet tall. The vast Yukon River ran along the land out to the Bering Sea and along the side of this small town of not quite 1,000 people. This waterway served as a "highway" of transportation for the bush villagers. In addition to the dreary houses among the bush, there were a couple of stores, a Laundromat, a police station, a clinic, a post office, a café and a school comprising the town we'd be staying in.

As we arrived at the large gray building that served as the church downstairs and the Joneses' home upstairs, Jennifer welcomed us with a hot breakfast of French toast. The sun began to shine, and Austin was anxious to begin painting. "Not quite the big city, is it?" Austin commented as he and I began spray painting the two-story building.

"Nope, not quite," I agreed, smiling. Austin reminded me a lot of myself when I was his age and first starting off at the reservation. I'd been so young, yet sure that God had great things in store for Corliss and me on that Indian reservation. God had been so faithful, and over the years had shown us exactly why he'd called us to those precious Native Americans. Austin and Jennifer had been obedient to the call as well, and I was excited to see what God would do in their lives up here.

Over a supper of again one of the most delicious pieces of salmon I'd ever tasted in my life, Austin filled us in a bit more on the culture of the bush. Emmonak was a fishing village; the people who lived there preferred to be called Yupik Eskimos. Because the area was so remote and food and supplies had to be flown in or come by boat, the price of food was astronomical. (A half gallon of ice cream cost as much as $14!) Consequently, most of the villagers ate (surprise!) fish for breakfast, lunch and dinner!

"There's not much to do out here," Austin admitted. "The teenagers kind of wander around on their four-wheelers, just hanging out and looking for ways to keep occupied. There are no video arcades or skating rinks to keep them busy. Consequently, drugs are a big problem up here. When the sun is out 24 hours a day during the summer, the days become very, very long."

The sidewalks were built out of wood planks two to four feet above the ground, and sewer pipes also ran above ground because of the permafrost. Electricity was unpredictable, as we experienced when the heat and lights went off in the middle of the day. We soon learned that e-mail was the best form of outside communication as our cell phones did not work up there.

Because the weather conditions were so harsh in the area, all of the buildings remained a dull gray color. The paint didn't stay on the weathered wood. Our job on this trip would be to give the church a fresh coat of paint that would not only brighten it up but protect the wood as well. I had purchased a paint sprayer from a Sherwin Williams store in Minot and had it shipped up to Anchorage. We would use the finest quality paint and hope that it would stay on the building for years to come.

Austin showed us the church where the three men would be staying in sleeping bags on air mattresses.

Living the Call

Corliss and I settled in for bed upstairs in the small spare bedroom. I had slept in everything from luxury hotels to rustic cabins to rundown motels over the years and was not especially picky about my accommodations. As long as I could get a decent night's sleep, I was happy. We were very comfortable. Austin and Jennifer were a good host and hostess, and their little boy, Aiden, kept us all entertained and made it impossible for all of us to not fall in love with him. "We're not in Minot anymore. Sweet dreams!" I joked to Corliss as we drifted off to sleep that evening.

We spent the next couple of days painting the church building, as well as installing new windows. I was pleased to see the paint stick to the wood and even happier to note what a difference the cheery warm tan color made in the appearance of the structure. The men also worked on building a deck between the house and Austin's shed where he kept his four-wheeler and his snowmobile. It was good to get these up above the mud. Austin was happy with the outcome as well. The next project was putting in new flooring in the kitchen and dining room upstairs. Because that project was in process, we all rode to the local restaurant in Austin's trailer for hamburgers for supper. The food tasted good even as we slid the old beat-up chairs up to the sagging table in the dimly lit restaurant with its dark and dingy wooden floor. It was quite an adventure!

Three of the guys went downriver the next day for more lumber. It was chilly (about 55 degrees) with a low pressure. We were at sea level, and sometimes we felt a little "woozy." Corliss, Jen and Aiden went to the store on the four-wheeler to get groceries. The next day we went downriver and painted Pastor Marvin's church at Alakanuk. Pastor Marvin was an Alaskan native. I enjoyed his company very much.

We discovered the electricity had been out while we were gone, and the ladies had eaten peanut butter sandwiches for dinner and played Scrabble in the dim light while Aiden took his nap. We had buffalo stew for supper, and the guys talked us all into playing cards to pass the time before we went to bed, pulling the curtains tight in our room to shut out the light.

"Mel, I want to take you out on the Yukon and show you one of our Bible camps," Austin told us one day. "You'll want a jacket, though. It gets pretty nippy out there." The ride upriver on the Yukon in Austin's 22-foot aluminum motorboat proved to be an unforgettable experience. We bounced up and down as the waves slapped against the side of the boat. The water misted our face as we flew over the choppy waters, amazed and invigorated by the vastness of the river and the beautiful scenery along the banks. What a fun experience for Loren, Craig, DelWayne, Corliss and me as Austin maneuvered the small boat up the Yukon River. Austin steered the boat conscientiously over the rough waters, being careful to dodge sandbars that might be underwater.

The Yukon River is a massive body of water. At seven miles across in places, it feels more like a large lake or even an ocean than a river. We saw two moose as we sped past the land; they looked quite at home in their rugged surroundings.

"Watch your step," Austin warned as he helped us out of the boat when we arrived at the camp. He threw us a rope, which we used to pull ourselves out of the boat and up the steep, muddy riverbank. I was thankful that we had our mud boots on!

I was amazed to see the unique setup of this campground. There were no buildings except for a small storage facility. When the people came here in the summer for their Bible camps, they brought tents to sleep in. What a precious time they must have worshipping together out in the middle of nature!

The next day Austin asked if we'd be willing to paint the church in the nearby village of Nunam Iqua where he went to hold services. The men agreed to go, but Austin was not comfortable to leave in the boat until the wind died down. Finally about 8 p.m., we loaded the paint sprayer into the boat and headed down the river once again. It was quite chilly and misty for a late August afternoon; the temperature dropped into the 50s. I was glad I had worn a sweatshirt and jeans. We told the ladies we would be back when it got totally light again.

By midnight, we had completed the paint job at the other church, and it was still light outside. It was hard to believe it was so late; my days and nights were completely thrown off because of it. We were just getting ready to leave when we heard a knock at the door of the church.

Alaska and Africa

"Can we come in?" About 14 young people stood at the door, looking for a place to hang out. We invited them in and had a great time of fellowship, talking, singing and sharing about the things of the Lord. They left around 2:30 a.m., and at 3:30 a.m., we started preparing to leave.

It was 4 a.m. by the time we climbed back into the boat and sped back up the Yukon. I was sleepy but also energized by the interesting night we'd just had. Suddenly, in the waters before us, a huge white whale leaped from the water and plunged back down again. The whale came up out of the water and went back down three more times. I sucked in my breath, unable to believe what we'd just seen. It was amazing so close up!

"He's fishing for salmon," Austin told me. "It is pretty common this time of the year."

"Wow! That was something," I replied. After unloading everything, we finally got back to the house about 6 a.m. Jennifer was worried, but after praying for us, Corliss said we must have decided to sleep before coming home.

The next day was Sunday, and the Emmonak church had a potluck fellowship meeting that evening. Several boatloads of people came from two other churches. Corliss and I had the pleasure of tasting some very unusual Alaskan food, including whale blubber, moose stew and even reindeer sausage. Aside from the blubber, everything was quite tasty. Of course, the smoked salmon was the best treat of all.

We thoroughly enjoyed the time of fellowship with the

native people. Most were warm and friendly, while some were very shy. The children ran around outside, laughing and playing with sticks or riding their bikes as the women and men waited for the service to begin inside. It was so neat to see people from such a different way of life serving and praising God in spite of their difficulties. I preached that evening in that humble little Alaskan church by the Yukon River to about 100 people. It was a time none of our group will ever forget.

After the people got back into their boats and headed down the river, someone brought some Alaskan "ice cream" up to the house for all of us. It didn't take long to figure out that this was not the kind of ice cream we are used to but was whitefish mashed together with mayonnaise! The taste will forever linger in my mind.

We thanked Austin and Jennifer for their hospitality before flying back to Anchorage with our friends. "I think I am actually going to miss you when you leave," Jennifer said as we gave goodbye hugs. What a brave and dedicated young couple they were. With three days remaining before we needed to return to Minot, our group decided we needed to do a little Alaskan sightseeing when we got back to Anchorage.

We all decided we wanted to take the one-day Glacier Cruise to Prince William Sound. We drove on Seward Highway, with Cook Inlet on one side, to the small quaint town of Whittier located on sea level at the base of the mountain. From there we boarded the Klondike Express and headed out into the water. The weather was cold, and

Alaska and Africa

rain was coming down. It was so cloudy and foggy we couldn't see anything. We all sat down at a table on board and began to pray. "Oh, Lord, you who have the power over the wind and the rain and the sky, would you please clear up the clouds and give us some sunshine so we can see the beauty of your creation today?"

Shortly after that, the clouds began to part, and the sun began to shine. The captain said on the loudspeaker at the beginning of the cruise that we would not be able to see much. At the end he said this was the best and clearest day they had had all summer! I thanked the Lord for answering our prayers. Sometimes we can forget that he cares about the smaller details of our lives, but clearly, he is listening all of the time.

That day, we saw 24 crystal-blue glaciers clinging from the edge of the snow-capped Chugach Mountains. Our cruise ship floated around there for a long time so people could absorb the awesome beauty and take pictures. Cute little sea otters popped up at the side of the boat as we went along, floating happily on their backs. We saw seals lying on floating chunks of ice, thousands of birds and other types of wildlife as well. We took a lot of pictures and enjoyed the food served on deck. It was a wonderful day!

We also traveled on to a wildlife reserve area, where we enjoyed seeing moose, reindeer, caribou, bear and other varieties of animals and birds. It was hard to believe we'd *tasted* some of those animals just a couple of days before! We learned that in Alaska, vegetables, flowers and other plants have a very short growing season but become huge and beautiful in such a short time because of the long days of light. The flowers in Anchorage were gorgeous.

The next day we took a day trip to Denali National Park. The native Alaskans in the towns along the way up told us they had not had a clear view of Mount McKinley for 30 days. However, we were able to get a good view of it on our way north. What a huge mountain peak! The tallest peak in North America, it towers over all the other mountains in the range and was perhaps one of the most beautiful sights I'd ever taken in. We explored lovely Denali National Park and bought CDs and calendars with pictures of the Northern Lights. As we drove farther up in the park, Craig and Loren decided to climb one of the huge rocks that boasted a climbing path. We took pictures of them from down below when we could actually spot them up on top!

Sarah Palin was governor of Alaska at the time. We drove through her hometown of Wasilla that day, not knowing that only a short time later she would be running for Vice President of the United States!

The next day everyone did some sightseeing and souvenir shopping in Anchorage. That evening the five of us went out for supper at a very nice restaurant with delicious food, Alaskan decorations and colorful totem poles before we all parted to fly out early the next morning. Visiting Alaska had been an experience none of us would ever forget, and we had had a great time together as a team as well.

Alaska and Africa

We took the "red eye" back to Minot and left at midnight Alaska time — 3 a.m. our time. We were tired by the time we got home due to jet lag, but we wouldn't have taken back a single moment. It had been a trip of a lifetime. We had experienced life in the Alaskan bush country, seen whales, moose and bear, made new friends and even eaten blubber! It would be nice to sleep in our own beds again and return to our routine. Little did we know, however, that another major adventure waited just around the corner.

Meanwhile, in September, 2008, Larry and Gloria Lundstrom joined us in Eagle Butte, South Dakota, for a major outreach on the Eagle Butte Indian Reservation Pow-Wow Grounds.

Convoy of Hope partnered with us to give out food and tons of clothing. The big tent was set up for ministry, and people flocked to the grounds. Hundreds of local volunteers arrived to get food set up to distribute and to sort clothing. Inflatable playground equipment was set up for the kids. Troy and Melena Dugan's semi-truck from Operation Outreach parked alongside the Convoy of Hope semi-truck loaded with goods waiting to be unpacked. Students from Trinity Bible College also came to work as volunteers in this huge project. We had great cooperation from the locals and figured we served about 3,700 people. Many people were prayed for at the ministry tent. We had boxes and boxes of literature that we gave to the Indian people who came to enjoy the music and preaching in the tent and became drawn to the Lord by the Holy Spirit. It was an exciting event, and only eternity will reveal all the results.

In January, 2009, we got another phone call. "Mel, you are going to go overseas and put up the new playground equipment for Jackson's Ridge Children's Training Center!" It was David Boyd from the U.S. missions BGMC department of the Assemblies of God in Springfield, Missouri. Through a BGMC program cooperating with Playtribe, I had been able to set up expensive playground equipment on Indian reservations here in the States. I was the only one trained to oversee this specific program, so I was the one chosen for this project. I was excited at the prospect, but first I had to find out just where this training center was.

"South Africa," Dave replied on the other end of the line. "It's just outside Johannesburg."

"Africa!" I exclaimed. Wow! I had never been to Africa. I agreed to begin getting the project off the ground, got off the phone and excitedly told Corliss the news.

"Africa!" she exclaimed. "Oh, my goodness!"

God once again proved faithful. Details and plans were worked out over the following weeks. Travel arrangements were completed for our team of six, comprised of Corliss and me and two young couples, Brian and Sara Lee and Rob and Andrea Lenertz. We were able to raise our funds and left with $8,000 cash and our airline tickets paid. Correspondence began between us and the missionaries at Jackson's Ridge.

We flew out of Minot on the 21st of March, 2009,

Alaska and Africa

landed in Atlanta, Georgia, flew across the Atlantic and touched down in Dakar, Senegal, to refuel. Corliss said to me in awe, "Mel, we are in Africa!"

"Halfway around the world!" I agreed. We then flew on to the city of Johannesburg. The total flight was nearly 22 hours.

We were weary and happy to have our reservations at the City Lodge in Johannesburg. To my surprise, the motel was gated and completely surrounded by a 12-foot-tall barbed-wire fence. Inside, however, the building was very nice with lovely comfortable rooms. I wondered why such a well-kept building would need to be gated. I soon got my answer.

We all decided we needed something to eat, and when we inquired about the best eating place, we were offered a ride in the motel van. "You can't travel or walk around here late at night by yourselves. It's not safe," we were told. We were told later that "downtown Johannesburg has been overtaken by criminals." While this great huge bustling metropolitan area of several million has the reputation of being a crime hub, it is also the economic heart of Africa.

"Thank you so much for letting us know," I replied as we gratefully accepted the ride to a fancy and delightful restaurant called Villa Bianca.

Johannesburg is one of the largest metropolitan cities in the world. With a population of nearly 4 million people, it bustles with large businesses and trade of all kinds. Though there are no major bodies of water surrounding the city, it is known for its mineral-rich hills, particularly gold and diamonds, which have contributed to the economic growth of the city over the years. It was hard to believe we were in the midst of a third-world country and not in New York.

The next morning, our missionary host, Ed Corbin, was there to load our suitcases and take us out to Jackson's Ridge Children's Training Center. Not more than a few miles outside of the city the scenery began to change drastically. Tin shacks replaced skyscrapers along the highway leading us to our destination. We stopped at a suburb along the way and ate lunch at the Mug and Bean. Corliss bought a red beaded necklace from a sidewalk vendor and paid the sweet African lady 30 rands, comparable to $3 in American money. Ed Corbin gave us a running brief all the way until we turned onto the rocky, bumpy dirt road that led us into Jackson's Ridge Camp. Eight-foot tall grass grew on each side of the road into the camp. The little one-lane road wound on for 26 miles. We had to be careful to avoid the rocks protruding in the middle of the road as we drove. The car bounced up and down as dust flew everywhere. It beat any roller coaster ride I'd ever been on!

When we finally arrived at Jackson's Ridge, we were impressed by the beauty of this peaceful place. Quaint brick buildings with thatched roofs were scattered about the spacious grounds.

We soon spotted monkeys swinging in the trees surrounding the compound. They swung from the roofs and the tree branches, treating their surroundings like their very own playground. While at first I found them cute, I would soon change my opinion about these goofy little creatures.

The campground could host up to 200 children who would come in for summer camps, staying in the large thatched dormitory with bunk beds stacked against the walls. African workers also came in for training camps in the summer. They had the opportunity to purchase puppets, books, CDs, literature and curriculum to share with the children they taught. There were no camps going on when we arrived, but work was being done on the grounds by the African workers. They were trimming trees, tending flower gardens, working on buildings and tending the horses in the barn. A type of palm tree grew outside the building where Corliss and I would be staying. Wild peacocks ran about in the back yard.

Ed and Sonja Corbin, Assemblies of God missionaries and directors of the camp, were our hosts. Ed gave us a tour of the grounds, and Sonja delighted us with a delicious get-acquainted dinner around the large table in their beautiful three-story thatched-roof home that evening. I could tell right away we were going to have a wonderful time. The Corbins' home was complete with many unique African curios and heads of animals that Ed had shot mounted on the walls. A curved stairwell leading to the upstairs bedrooms and Ed's office on the third floor was made out of railroad ties. Mrs. Corbin, who preferred to be called Sonja, bought groceries for us to prepare breakfast and lunch for ourselves each day in the "Joel and Casey" house where the two young couples on our team stayed. However, she informed us she would be making dinner for us each evening at their house after a long day's work.

One evening after dinner in our prayer meeting with about 20 of the workers there, I shared my testimony of how God had called me to the Indian people. "I pleaded with God, asking him why he couldn't send me to a foreign country like Africa or India, but he chose to keep me close to home, working with the Native Americans on the Indian reservation," I explained.

Corliss, who was sitting beside me on the couch, slapped me on my knee abruptly and exclaimed, "Mel, you are in Africa!" Indeed, I was! It had taken many years to get here, but God had sent me to Africa after all. We chuckled, and I continued to share my testimony about the many good things God had done in our lives over the years.

Our team discussed the logistics of the playground project. There was much work to be done in a short period of time, but I was confident we could complete it. The playground project had a slightly rough start. The cement truck arrived to pour the cement, but we quickly realized there wasn't going to be enough ready-mix. We were told that no other trucks would be coming back in that day. If we didn't get all the cement poured at the same time, the result could be disastrous. I began to think quickly.

"Sir, is there any way you could get another cement

truck in here today?" we asked. We pulled out 100 rands; 30 rands equaled $3. One hundred rands was equivalent to several days' wages in South Africa. The man's eyes lit up when he saw the money.

"I'll be right back!" he replied swiftly and roared off in his truck. The man returned as promised, and we were able to pour the rest of the cement that day.

This wasn't the only challenge we would encounter. Playtribe had shipped parts for three different types of playgrounds, which meant we had to draw up a new plan to follow. The process was tedious as we put together large pieces of green and white tubular steel stands and screwed in hundreds of screws. We worked diligently from morning till evening to complete the 40x80-foot structure, which in the end fit together perfectly, was functional and looked beautiful!

It was mid-March and very hot in this area; from 10 a.m. to 4 p.m. the sun beat down on us as we worked. Sweat ran off our backs, and sunburns became bright red if we forgot our hats. Corliss kept reminding us to drink a lot of water so that we wouldn't get dehydrated. Ed had given me a Gator four-wheeler to drive around the property from the building site to the garage and back to the house where we ate as a team. It was a lifesaver — it sure beat walking! I could not have walked far in that heat around the large campgrounds.

Herman, a quiet, older, totally dedicated tall dark African man whom we grew to love, was in charge of the grounds. I had brought several power tools with me, which came in very handy during the project, as their tools were old and limited. He was impressed and enjoyed working with us, helping us find things in their old dusty garage.

The young African men were helpful and interested. They came alongside us as we built, giving invaluable assistance. A young energetic African man named Bootie became a fast friend. We enjoyed his sense of humor and engaging smile. He worked hard and diligently, watching closely as we pulled out various tools to work with. I was equally intrigued by his native tongue, Swahili. He and the other men frequently conversed back and forth rapidly, while we listened, hoping to learn perhaps a word or two.

The women were equally helpful. Two native women, Constance and Demetria, assisted Sonja at the house throughout the day. They did cleaning, helped prepare the meals and even washed and folded our clothes. One day, Corliss talked with one of the women and thanked her for her kindness. "Ooh, we love to do it," Demetria replied sweetly. "It is a ministry for us."

That evening Corliss said to Sonja, "Is this 'paradise lost' or what? It is beautiful here, and our clothes are washed and folded for us with love, and our rooms are cleaned each day!" Sonja just smiled.

At the end of one long, hot day, Corliss went for a dip in the little swimming pool just outside our house beyond the veranda. Swarms of wasps surrounded the pool, but Corliss prayed, "Lord, you protected Daniel in the lion's den. Please protect me as well!" So she jumped in to cool off, and those wasps never bothered her. The ladies repeated this welcome reprieve after several long hot days.

There were a number of horses in the barn for the children to ride during camp. Sara and Andrea took advantage of the sport and went horseback riding. We came to know soft-spoken Jaa, who took care of the barn and horses. In front of the house where Corliss and I stayed were beautiful huge palm trees and a rose bush garden, as well as other foliage, which were taken care of by native groundskeepers. Each person had his or her specific assignments. The playground would add great fun to this camp for children who had little or nothing at home.

While our accommodations were beautiful, it was easy to forget we were still in a third-world country. Electricity was quite a problem on the property. One evening during a huge thunder and rainstorm, the electricity was out for a long time. This happened often, which meant we had to make the most of those hours. Phone service was limited, but we did have Internet service at the office to send e-mail to the people back home and let our families know how we were doing.

Each evening after we freshened up, it was a joy to jump on our Gator and ride over to the Corbin house for a delectable meal that Sonja had prepared. We had a delightful time visiting and swapping stories at the end of a meal and enjoyed one another's company. One evening we had a "brae" out on their veranda. Ed grilled wild meat, ostrich, chicken, wildebeest and wurst outdoors on the cement fire pit. Sonja pulled the curtains around the eating area as the cool of the night came on. It was a cozy feeling, even though we were eating half a world away from our home in Minot, North Dakota.

One evening, a bat entered the Corbins' house and began flying around. Ed took out his .22 pistol and promptly shot at the creature. We chuckled at his swift response to the unwelcome intruder. As a former farm boy, I thought I had seen it all, but apparently I hadn't!

At last, the playground was completed. Because we had pieced together three different playgrounds, it was a Jackson's Ridge Special. But it looked great. We leveled truckloads of sand beneath the structure and stood back to admire it. Friday morning, we dedicated it to the Lord with all the workers who had helped build it. I imagined 200 children happily climbing on it during summer camp later this year. What a good time they would have!

We also built a stage in the Owen-Carr Center, the large main auditorium. The stage was built so that their puppets could come up on the stage from the floor below. I had a hunch it would be a big hit with the kids.

Since our team had booked our visit for just more than two weeks, we had a few days to sightsee. We had asked Ed to schedule a non-shooting African safari for us. We went on the Mankeve Safari Heritage Tour at Pilanesberg. As we drove along in our open-topped vehicle, our guide suddenly whipped around and tore down another road. There one of the biggest elephants we had ever seen had planted himself in the middle of the road. No vehicles got around him on either side! We quietly watched as baby elephants and elephants of all sizes came ambling out of the brush. Our tour guide told us there were at least 40 elephants in the herd. As we drove through the 55,000-acre game reserve, we also saw giraffes, antelopes, wildebeests, water buffalo, rhinoceroses, warthogs and even seven different kinds of zebras in their natural habitat. Who knew there were so many types of zebras? What an interesting trip it was!

That same day we also visited the beautiful and famous Sun City, with its hotels, casinos, shops and restaurants, and ate lunch at the buffet there. We viewed the Palace of the Lost City and the man-made Valley of Waves, walked through its stunning botanical gardens of flowers and foliage, over bridges and through a bird sanctuary, where a beautiful red bird stopped to perch on my shoulder! We enjoyed the larger-than-life atmosphere of this opulent resort. Later on in the afternoon, we had the unique privilege of petting some 3-month-old baby lions.

On a hot Sunday morning we attended a local church service. Ed Corbin was a good friend of the pastor, and several people from Jackson's Ridge attended this particular church as well. We enjoyed these warm, energetic people in the service. At the beginning of the service, they danced, sang and swayed with all of their might in front of the stage. At last, the pastor stood up and announced, "If you don't go sit down, we will never be able to get on with this service!"

Corliss and I laughed, as we were always encouraging

people to feel free to express themselves in church services. Oh, what we would have given to have to say those words to some of our reserved congregations in the upper Midwestern part of the United States!

The church service turned out to be somewhat of a political event. The presidential candidate Zuma of South Africa happened to be attending that Sunday, and a large entourage had followed him into the church. A political speech took place during part of the service, while helicopters buzzed overhead afterward. I had the pleasure of shaking hands with the president that morning as he left down the aisle where we were sitting — something I won't forget.

Our team of six and the Corbins were the only white people in the building that morning. A little boy sat with his parents in the row in front of us. He was fascinated with my white hair and proceeded to come over and climb into my lap. We became fast friends right away!

After church and lunch, the Corbins took us to an African bartering craft market. After being accosted quite a few times to buy this and buy that, Corliss became quite the bargainer. We bought souvenirs for our kids and a canvas picture of an African scene for a few rands. Everything was very inexpensive in American money.

We also visited a cultural center the next day. Our guide, dressed in sleek furs and skins, told us about the country and the activities that made its culture unique. As we strolled down the sidewalk later that day, two adorable little girls in beautiful beaded headdresses and costumes came running up behind us. "Take us to America with you!" they cried out.

"Okay, I will, I will," Corliss replied, laughing. She fished her camera out of her purse and had me take a picture of her with her two new friends.

At last, our missions trip of a lifetime came to an end. It was time to say goodbye to the Corbins and our other new friends at Jackson's Ridge. We packed our belongings, leaving behind a trunk of tools I'd brought from the States. I glanced around Jackson's Ridge one last time, taking in the beauty of the campground and the many memories that we had made in the past two weeks. And then it was time to head back down that bumpy dirt road, out to the highway and on to Johannesburg to fly out.

As our plane ascended into the air, I reflected on the excitement of the past few months. As home missionaries, we had never imagined we'd ever travel outside of the immediate United States. Yet our travels had taken us from the bush of Alaska all the way to the bustling city of Johannesburg, South Africa, and Jackson's Ridge camp within two years. We'd seen God working in a tiny church of Eskimos, as well as in a large, vivacious church of Africans. And we'd been able to put our practical skills to use, helping other missionaries, while at the same time building new relationships and seeing parts of the world we might not have otherwise ventured to. Both were trips of a lifetime, and we would be forever grateful for the experiences.

Our life had been many things over the years. It had

been difficult yet rewarding, stretching yet enjoyable. But one thing was for certain: It had definitely not, for even a moment, been dull!

Bush taxi

MAPS team in Alaska

Alaska and Africa

New deck we installed

Sewer and water lines above ground in the bush

Living the Call

Boat trip on the Yukon River

Corliss and Austin on the Yukon River

Alaska and Africa

Mel and Corliss, Alaska

Alaskan glacier

Living the Call

Alaskan glacier

Mel and Corliss in Africa

Alaska and Africa

MAPS team in Africa

Building the playground

Living the Call

Elephant blocking the road on our African safari

Elephant herd on our African safari

Alaska and Africa

Giraffes on our African safari

Giraffes on our African safari

Living the Call

Zebras on our African safari

Mel petting a lion cub

Alaska and Africa

Playground

Team at Jackson's Ridge SA

Living the Call

Playground

Kids and camp on playground

Chapter Ten
All Things Work Together
For Good

Many of us are familiar with the Bible verse Romans 8:28: "In all things God works for the good of those who have been called according to his purpose." It has always been a favorite of mine, but in this past year, the words have taken on a special meaning for Corliss and me.

I continued with my position as Special Projects Coordinator with U.S. missions of the Assemblies of God. We had built more than 20 churches around the country; it was exciting to see God's work taking place on Indian ground. One of our most recent projects was a Hogan building in Pinedale, New Mexico. The pastor on the reservation wanted to build a parsonage in the shape of an octagon that would closely resemble the other Indian buildings. We had never built a Hogan before; I thought it would be interesting to do something so unusual.

In the fall of 2009, I headed down to New Mexico to help finish the Hogan building. My plan was to stop in Denver, Colorado, where I would pick up my friend Brian. Brian had assisted me on many of the church building projects and would be working with me on this one as well.

One of our friends had given me a beautiful 1998

Living the Call

Lincoln Town Car to donate to the missionaries in New Mexico. On a chilly Saturday afternoon, just two days after Thanksgiving, I climbed into the Lincoln and set off for the long drive to New Mexico.

I had spent a considerable amount of time on the road the past few years and was accustomed to driving the long trips. I used the time to pray and think when I drove alone. I was enjoying the beautiful scenery just north of Buffalo, South Dakota, when a huge buck came tearing out of the darkness into the light of the headlights and ran straight into my path! There was no time to steer out of the way; I hit him — or rather, he hit me! — dead on and pushed me into the right ditch.

I tried to catch my breath while the car came to a stop as I steered it back on to the edge of the road. Both airbags had deployed at the moment of impact. I slowly untangled myself from the seat and climbed out of the car to assess the damage. The bumper was completely ripped off, and the entire left side of the car was dented in. I then glanced over at the road, where the buck lay sprawled out, dead. It was a sad scene, but I was thankful at the moment just to be alive. I had always prayed for God to keep animals off of the road whenever I drove, as I knew how dangerous it could be if they collided with my car.

To my relief, the car was still running. I took off some of the broken parts and managed to drive down the road to Buffalo, where I headed to a gas station to call the sheriff. After 45 minutes, a sheriff arrived and assessed the scene of the accident.

All Things Work Together For Good

"He did a good number on your car, didn't he?" the sheriff quipped as he walked around the vehicle.

"Yes, it sure did," I replied as I removed some more of the damaged pieces of plastic off the car. I opened up the trunk to make sure the contents were okay. I had put a heavy cast-iron sink in the trunk; I planned to install it in the new church parsonage in New Mexico. Everything seemed to be intact. "I'm free to go on now?" I asked, climbing back in the car.

"Yes, sir! You be careful out there now."

I heeded his words, driving extra vigilantly as I headed to Belle Fourche, South Dakota, to spend the night before heading to Colorado. Brian was waiting for me in downtown Denver; I filled him in on the accident as we drove. "I feel bad that the car's not going to be in good shape for the missionaries when we arrive," I lamented. "At least it's still drivable."

We stopped at a Home Depot in Colorado Springs to pick up some building supplies. Brian volunteered to drive for the next leg of the trip, and I gladly took him up on his offer. We were just leaving Alamosa, Colorado, when Brian promptly turned the car around. "What are you doing?" I asked him, sitting up in my seat.

"I saw a Lincoln Town Car back in that lot," he said excitedly. "Let's go check it out!"

We pulled into the used car lot to inspect the car. Sure enough, there sat a Lincoln Town Car that looked much like the one we were driving (minus the damage!). A closer look confirmed it was a year newer than the one we were driving. It was nearly 7 p.m. on Sunday and the lot was closed, but we took down the number of the dealer and decided to call on the car first thing in the morning.

The next morning, we called the dealer right away. He explained that a man had brought the car in on consignment the day before. The owner had purchased it for his wife, who had driven it only during the day. It had been garaged most of the time and was in immaculate condition. I couldn't believe it! Some might have called it coincidence or good luck, but I knew better.

"Would you take $5,000 for it?" Brian asked.

"How about $6,000?" the dealer countered.

We agreed that the price was fair, and we returned to the lot to purchase the car. I then called my insurance company to tell them about the accident. I explained that though the car was being donated to a missionary family, my name was on the sticker. They sent out an adjuster to inspect the damage before we left. Brian drove the new car, and I followed behind in the old one. We must have looked quite a sight, two Lincoln Town Cars driving down the road, one in tip-top shape and one on its last leg! I thanked God for his amazing provision. I had no idea how things would all work out financially, but I was sure God would provide, as he had done so many times before.

The damaged Lincoln began overheating, but we managed to make it to Albuquerque, New Mexico, without any other setbacks. I was weary as we reached our motel. I picked up the phone to call the pastor of the church. "We're here!" I announced. "We'll see you in an

All Things Work Together For Good

hour to go out to eat. And we have another little surprise for you, too."

That evening we gave them a ride in the new car that they did not realize was going to be theirs. We then had the pleasure of handing the keys of the Lincoln over to the pastor and his wife. We told him the story in its entirety, and he was thrilled. "I can't believe it! This car is beautiful! It will be so useful for our family," he said gratefully.

We finished working on the Hogan over the next three days. I was pleased to see it had turned out so nicely. This design was a first for us, but I wondered if other reservation churches in the Southwest would take notice and want to replicate it. After our project was complete, the pastor drove Brian and me back to the airport in Albuquerque. From there, we parted ways; Brian returned to Denver, and I went back to Minot. It had certainly been a memorable trip.

Once back in Minot, I got a call from the insurance company. "We are able to give you $6,800 for the Lincoln," they informed me.

I couldn't believe the good news! I had a $500 deductible, and some repairs we had made to the vehicle. After all was said and done, we had to pay about $1,500 for the 1999 Lincoln. God was so faithful! What could have ended in disaster and disappointment had ended up perfectly in a happy surprise. Corliss was delighted with this story when I told her, and said, "You can't tell me that God wasn't in this one!" One of the interesting things is that there were many new parts and tires on the wrecked one that fit on the 1999, and we bought it back so they could have the extra items. He had truly worked all things together for good.

After the first of the year, I headed off to Big Sky, Montana, for a ski trip with my brother Don. I had enjoyed skiing in Colorado and Montana many times over the years and was looking forward to celebrating my birthday on the slopes and spending time with Don, my two nephews and my brother's grandson.

We skied all day Monday. It was a beautiful day; the sun splashed across the white powder as I skied down the mountain more than 15 times. The next morning, I stayed back with my brother at his condo to cook up a big batch of chili. We then hit the slopes about 10 a.m. We were going down for lunch about 11:30.

I was just about down the mountain when a snowboarder flew by on my left and cut me off. I turned abruptly to avoid colliding with him, and as I did, my boot came out of my ski. I fell very slowly to the snow, and as I fell, I felt and heard my leg break!

When I sat up and looked at my foot, it was at a right angle to my leg. I knew that was not good. I couldn't take looking at it that way, so I sat up and put my boot with my foot in it back into line. I knew without a doubt that it was broken.

I lay back on the snow and heard the Lord clearly say to me, "All things work together for good to those who love God and are called according to his purpose."

I said, "Okay, Lord, I am going to find out the good in

this!" These words would echo in my mind over and over in the days and weeks to come.

A skier stopped and asked if I was okay; then he called the ski patrol. Within minutes, help was there. Two ski patrol personnel arrived by my side to assess my condition. "How's your head? Your shoulders? Can you see straight? How did you fall?" The questions came one after another.

"My head's fine, my shoulders are fine," I replied. "It's my leg. I know it's broken."

Two paramedics arrived and took my blood pressure and pulse. "It's my leg," I assured them, growing a bit impatient. "Everything else on me is fine."

They put my leg into a splint and moved me onto the sled to take me down the mountain slope, but they quickly realized they couldn't get enough momentum. So they called for a snowmobile, which pulled the sled and me down the mountain. A swift 20 minutes from the time of my fall, I was sitting in the first aid station next door to the Big Sky Clinic, where I was soon sent for an x-ray.

"It's broken for sure," the x-ray technician confirmed after the first x-ray.

"I knew that," I replied, sighing. After the second x-ray, they told me it was so bad I would be having surgery in Bozeman, Montana, that evening!

"I want to take two more x-rays. It's not going to cost you anything," the tech added. "I want them for my 'Incredible' file!"

"Okay," I said, "so it's that bad!"

Living the Call

The ski resort was nice enough to refund all my money for my entire ski trip. My brother drove me to the nearest hospital in the city of Bozeman. I had broken my leg in six different places. The doctors wanted to operate on it right away. The top orthopedic surgeon at the hospital was available to perform the surgery at 6:30 that night. Everything was happening too quickly. I was grateful for everyone's quick response, but I wanted to make some phone calls home before I got to the hospital in Bozeman.

Corliss was at work, and I was unable to get hold of her. I called Rhonda on my way to Bozeman. She was also on her way to work, so she called Shawna, who went to the house and told Corliss when she got off work. Corliss was frustrated and angry to the point of tears, but toughened up by the time we talked on the phone before I went into surgery. She asked me to have the surgeon call her when the surgery was over.

I praise God for being conscious as the doctors slid me onto the operating table. Just before I lost consciousness, I raised my hand and prayed out loud, "Lord, please be with these doctors and nurses as they go into this surgery."

"You didn't pray for yourself," the staff observed when I finished my prayer.

"I know where I'm going if I die," I replied. "But I don't know about the rest of you!"

A friend from Kulm was heading out to ski in Montana that same week. Our friend Garth from Minot agreed to catch a ride out with this man and come and take me back to Minot, North Dakota, after the surgery.

All Things Work Together For Good

When I awoke, I was groggy but in no pain. My leg had been propped up with five pillows, and an external stabilizing fixture had been pinned into the bones of my leg to keep it in place. I was instructed to keep my leg above my heart at all times to avoid blood clots. I had to keep it completely elevated with not an ounce of pressure on it. It was going to be a long road to recovery.

Garth drove me back to Minot a day later; I slept in the back seat most of the way home. This was the quickest ride across Montana that I have ever had. I was happy to see Corliss once we arrived, and she was more than relieved to see me. I slept in the living room recliner chair, and at 7:30 the next morning, we went for an appointment with an orthopedics doctor at Trinity Hospital in Minot. He had bad news.

"You've had six major breaks in your left leg between your knee and your ankle," he explained, examining the x-rays. "I'd like to do another surgery next Tuesday."

The following Tuesday, I went in for another surgery. Just before the doctors went to operate, I raised my hands and prayed as I had in the hospital in Montana. Again, the doctors asked why I had prayed only for them and not myself.

"I know where I'm going, but I don't know about the rest of you," I replied with a smile.

A nursing assistant came into my room after midnight to check on me. "Were you by chance a missionary to the Indians?" she asked quietly.

I nodded. "Yes, I was."

Living the Call

"Did you do an outreach in Eagle Butte in 2008?"

"Yes, I did."

Tears filled her eyes as she spoke. "I accepted the Lord into my life at that outreach! My life has not been the same since!" I was so happy to hear that this woman had come to know the Lord at one of our outreaches. What a blessing to meet someone who had been touched by our ministry and know she was walking strong with him. And how exciting to be under the care of another believer! God had truly placed me in good hands.

I spent the entire week recovering in the hospital. January 15th arrived; it was my 65th birthday. Though there were a hundred other places I would have rather spent my big day, I made the best of the situation. Lynelle sent me the game "Sorry," which seemed amusingly appropriate. My family also brought balloons, cards, flowers and a cookie bouquet, which helped brighten up the hospital room. My strong faith in God and my supportive family kept me from slipping into pity mode.

Once I returned home, Corliss' nursing skills kicked into full gear. I had to sit in my recliner all night and day, keeping my leg propped up on pillows above my heart. I could only get up to go to the bathroom. Corliss brought me my meals and sat by my side to keep me company. She also administered the shots I needed to prevent blood clots. Home health nurses came in every few days to change my bandages. Though I was sometimes in a great deal of pain, I decided to be a good patient and make the best of my situation.

All Things Work Together For Good

I had yet another surgery a month later. Once again, just before I went under, I repeated my prayer for the doctors and nurses, asking God to guide them and touch them. During this four-hour surgery, I had a 14-inch metal plate put into my leg, attached with 13 screws. I also needed some cadaver bone to help the bones heal together. The doctor told Corliss, who was anxiously waiting in the waiting room, that it took a whole team to get this leg set in place. The doctor chose to put my leg in a splint instead of a cast, so I could not put any weight on it for the next 12 weeks!

I took a long time to come out of anesthesia. When I did, I was very groggy and disoriented. I called for one of the doctors. "Did you tell me I made a mess out of my leg, or did I dream that?" I asked, rubbing my eyes.

The doctor laughed and said, "No, I said that to the nurse in the recovery room," he replied, smiling. "You weren't supposed to hear that!"

I must be the talk of the hospital, I thought to myself as I drifted back to sleep.

I returned home and continued to recover slowly. We were extremely thankful to find out that all of our medical expenses had been covered. As missionaries who had not had health insurance for the past five years, things could have been quite catastrophic for us. God was so faithful to provide for all of our needs. What a relief to not have to worry about hospital bills during a time like this.

One morning after church, however, Corliss broke down to our daughter Rhonda. "No one is going to continue to support a missionary who can't do anything but sit with his leg up all day," she cried. "What are we going to do?"

After a good cry and a stiff lecture from Rhonda, Corliss composed herself. She had been such a faithful partner over the years in the midst of my many accidents and health problems. She was quickly reminded that God had taken care of us during each of those times and would continue to do so in our future. Things might never be the same going forward, but somehow, we would make it.

Though I was still fully confined to my recliner, I began to realize that I could do a great deal of work from home.

"I think I can still carry on a lot of these special projects right here in our living room," I told Corliss. "I've got my cell phone, e-mail and my laptop computer. What more do I need?"

And so, in the weeks to come, Corliss set up my "home office" right there in our living room. I began making phone calls, letting everyone know I was still on board as Special Projects Coordinator. Brian, my friend who had accompanied me to New Mexico, assured me that he could step in as my right-hand man. He would prove to be a huge help to me over the next few months.

One Friday, we got a phone call from our headquarters in Springfield. They had accidentally overpaid us on our last support check and needed to retract half the pay. This was a huge blow to us financially. We had no idea how we were going to pay our pending bills for the next few weeks,

All Things Work Together For Good

as we had already paid current bills with the check we had gotten.

I had been reading the book of Job in the Bible since I came home from the hospital. Though he had been a righteous man, Job endured more trials than most ever will in a lifetime. I had decided that I would not throw myself a pity party after reading about Job. However, the day we got that phone call, I couldn't help but mutter, "Job, I feel your pain."

On Tuesday the following week, I was working on my laptop when it promptly crashed. The laptop was my livelihood and my link to the outside world! I had all my data on it, and I had no idea if it was retrievable. I called up tech support, and a man came to the house and was able to retrieve the data on the hard drive. Thank the Lord! Still, it was one more trial on top of everything else we were going through. Could we bear any more?

The answer was yes. Some weeks later, I was sitting in my recliner when I heard a noise in the basement. Determined to find out what it was, I slid down the steps to the basement on my behind. After looking around a bit, I discovered that the water softener had sprung a leak. "Job, I'm feeling more of your pain," I mumbled, grimacing.

Then one morning, Corliss and I woke up shivering. It was 55 degrees in the house! The furnace man came and said, "I have some good news and some bad; which would you like first?"

I replied, "The bad!" He discovered that the heat

exchanger on the furnace had cracked. I asked him what the good news was, and he told me he could come on Tuesday and put in a new furnace.

I had been a good sport throughout the entire broken leg incident and all the other trials, but this was one more time when God spoke to me and said, "All things work together for GOOD!!!"

Things began looking up in the next week. We were able to get someone out to put in a new furnace, and God was once again faithful to provide financially. Like Job, we had been put to the test. I was thankful we had the Lord and each other to lean on during these trials. He had never once let us down, and even when we'd thought we could not go on, he'd been behind us all along.

I shared very honestly about our trials in our monthly newsletter to our supporters. I wanted them to know that we were indeed human and had to rely on God to get us through the difficult times. I was touched by the outpouring of support we received from everyone. While a few people wrote to ask, "Why hasn't God healed you yet?" I knew that in his timing, he would. The pastoral staff at our church in Minot was so supportive as well. They anointed me with oil and prayed for me, asking the Lord to fully heal my leg.

I began going to physical therapy three times a week. I tried to keep up a cheerful spirit, joking with the office staff and the physical therapists during my visits. One lady next to me had broken her leg six weeks after me and was always moaning and groaning about her situation. I told

All Things Work Together For Good

her what had happened to me, how I had broken my leg in six different places and had a 14-inch plate put in. I hoped that my positive attitude might be contagious. She said, "I guess I don't have much to complain about."

The next few weeks were full of little "graduations." I first graduated from the hospital to my recliner, next from the recliner to a walker, then to two crutches and finally to one crutch. One day soon, I was determined to walk with no crutches at all. And I was even more determined to hit the ski slopes once again someday, too!

In December, just before I went on my ski trip, I had spoken with a man named Daren Lindley on the phone. Daren shared about his ministry, Good Book Publishing. He told me to let him know if I was ever interested in publishing a book about our adventures as missionaries to the Indians. I had enjoyed talking with Daren but put our conversation on the back burner when life got busy.

Now, as I sat in my recliner with more time on my hands, I began to revisit the idea of writing that book. I gave Daren a call again, and we discussed moving forward with the project. Corliss became excited about it as well; she agreed it was a great time to finally put our stories into a book.

After Corliss shared at a women's retreat that we would finally be writing our book, our friend Sister Bakke threw back her head and laughed. "So God had to allow Mel to break his leg so he could finally get this book written!"

Corliss shared this conversation with me, and I began

to think about those words I'd heard the Lord say to me when I'd first heard my leg snap on the ski slope: "All things work together for good to those who love God and are called according to his purpose." It had been a hard road, but God had indeed worked all things together for good in this situation. Had I not broken my leg, I'm not sure we would have ever made the time to sit down and write this book. And I am confident God wanted us to share the many stories of his healing, forgiveness, provision and protection that we have experienced over the 40-plus years we've been in ministry. Our prayer is that others will be inspired to trust in him and live their own lives by faith as they read about God's call on our lives and his faithfulness through all these experiences.

Corliss and I have traveled halfway around the world and back, have seen miracle upon miracle take place and witnessed many giving their lives to the Lord. We have cried, laughed and rejoiced with the many people God has put in our lives over the years. From the people on the reservation to the kind doctors and nurses who treated me in the hospital, our own lives have been touched by too many to name. We have also endured heartache, loss, sadness and frustration. But in those moments, God has remained the same: faithful, loving and ever present. We've taken the good along with the bad and would not trade it for anything in the world. Life in the ministry is an adventure. We remain in God's hands, looking forward to what God is going to do in the future as we live out his call on our lives.

Conclusion

As we pulled together the stories of our lives during the past two decades, we found God to be just as amazing now as in the beginning. After Mel broke his leg, we discovered God wanted us to use this year as a time of convergence and share with you the stories written in this book.

As we move into the second half of the path of life, our ministry is ongoing. We desire to be faithful to God's call in preaching the word and warning people to have their hearts right with Christ before his soon return. People need Jesus, and we want to be a part of that great ingathering of souls.

We would like to share with you the ABCs of Salvation card that we have distributed by the thousands. If you have not asked Christ into your life, follow these steps and pray this simple prayer for salvation:

"Lord Jesus, I am a sinner, and I believe that you died for my sins. I believe that you rose again and are alive today listening to my prayer. Forgive me and save me from my sins. I accept you as my Savior. Thank you for promising me eternal life with you." (See John 3:16.)

Be encouraged to live for the Lord Jesus Christ. The Bible is his written word to us. Read it and study it. In it you will find true direction for life. Find and have fellowship with Christians in a Bible-believing church.

Living the Call

You may log on to our Dakota Missionary Evangelism Web site, dakotame.com, to keep in touch. Feel free to contact us. Our Web site is interactive. May God bless you as you embark on the adventures God has for you!

ABCs OF SALVATION

A-Acknowledge that you are a sinner
(Romans 3:23; Romans 6:23)
B-Believe that Jesus is Lord and that God raised him
from the dead (Romans 10:9; John 3:16)
C-Confess (ask forgiveness) with your mouth and
verbalize your belief (Romans 10:9)

A BASIC PLAN OF SALVATION

*Romans 3:23 - All people are sinners
*Romans 5:8 - Christ died to save us
*Romans 6:23 - Sin earns death, but God wants
to give us eternal life in Christ
*Romans 10:9 - A person must believe in Christ
and confess Christ as Savior
*Romans 10:13 - This Gift of salvation is
claimed through prayer
*1 John 2:3-4 - Proof of salvation is obedience

GOOD BOOK
PUBLISHING
www.goodbookpublishing.com